Computing Texts

A C++ notebook

A first course in programming

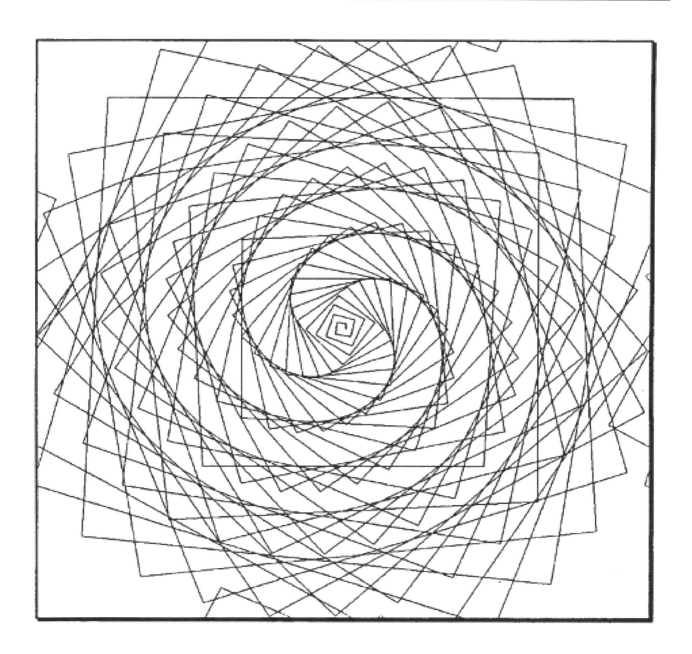

Tony Hawken

ISBN 978-1-4452-4340-5

Preface

Aim

The aim of this book is to introduce structured programming to students who possibly haven't programmed before. The vehicle chosen for this, is the C++ programming language. It is primarily designed for a short course at college, and is intended to have the level of difficulty of a level 3 course such as A' level in computing, a BTEC National in IT or a computing course for an Access Diploma.

I should also note that the book covers the same sort of level at programming as the course "Programming Methodology", that is currently taught in the first year at the University of Westminster on their BSc Computer Science program.

Origins

Quite a number of years ago, I started teaching computing on an Access to Higher Education course. The language used at the time was Pascal. Even then I considered this choice of language outdated and inappropriate. I wanted a language that students would continue to use at university, or would at least provide transferable skills. Then as now, both C++ and Java tended to be the language of choice for a first course in programming at university. The dominant language in universities is currently Java, but there are many similarities in the languages.

I chose C++, because I wanted the students to work in a simple environment. At the time, this was not possible for Java. When I first started teaching C++, I was obliged to use the old standard, as the only software available at the college was Turbo C++ for DOS. Now it is very easy to obtain a variety of free IDEs for C++. I chose Quincy 2005, as it is one of the simplest to use.

The course I taught followed the procedural paradigm, as we had to cover the same sort of topics that was in the Pascal course. All we did was change occurrences of Pascal to C++. Later on when a rewrite was necessary for the 3 modules of programming validated by OCN, it was possible to change the modules so that it looked more like a C++ course.

Once I discovered Quincy 2005, I totally rewrote my notes. This had the advantage that the notes were now ANSI compliant, but only for a very small part of the language. They had also grown in size considerably. It is largely these notes that this book is based.

Approach

The material in this book is designed to be informal and easy to use. It is a very practical "How to do" book, where the emphasis is trying things out. There is very little theory – just enough, in my opinion to make sense. The bulk of the book is made up of example programs with brief notes to explain how the programs work.

There are in some cases introductory notes that appear before the example programs, and there are exercises to work from in addition.

There are 3 parts to this book. Each part corresponds to a module taught on the Access to Computing course. These parts are divided up into 5 chapters or weeks. Each chapter should take a week to complete. This involves 3 hours of teaching per week in college, and between 2 and 3 hours homework per week. The 3 hours teaching per week at college should involve about 40% practical work writing programs, the remainder being used for lecture.

There is possibly too much material in the book. This is intentional, as it provides more scope for the more able student. Any teacher who adopts this book for use in a class should be aware of this. It is possible that they will choose to omit sections. The extra material will allow for differentiated teaching.

Resources

The Quincy 2005 IDE is Open Source software. That is, it is not only free to use, but developers can modify the software. I decided to use this software, because I wanted my students to have access to the same software used in college, on their computer at home.

Besides this, the central software to be used for the course, I can further suggest other Open Source software, that would be useful for such a student. The first of these is OpenOffice. This is produced by Sun Microsystems, and is very similar to Microsoft Office, only much more compatible. It can open various versions of Microsoft Word. You can choose to save in many different formats, including just about all the versions of Microsoft Word. It is much more compatible with Microsoft Word, than any of the versions of Word, and much less annoying. Despite being a long-term Word user, I have been forced to use OpenOffice for this book. The diagrams, such as structure charts were redrawn using the drawing tool of OpenOffice, as the results were much better.

Where mathematical typesetting was required, I have used another open source product called WinTexmacs. Lastly, I have extensively used Microsoft Paint to crop my screen dumps that were obtained by pressing Print screen.

This book makes no pretences at being complete, and in many cases may be too brief. For that reason, it is recommended that other books are consulted – see the bibliography for suggestions.

Contents

Part 2   Further C++ Programming

Part 3 Arrays, Structures and text file processing

Part 1

Basic programming skills in C++

Aims

After completing this 5-week unit, you will be able to do the following:

Data

Describe the different data types available in C++, explaining how they can be used.

Declare and use variables. Use of variables includes assignment and applying arithmetic operators to them.

Input and output

Write simple working programs that include suitable input and output that is suitably formatted.

Control structures

Identify and use appropriate selection methods to solve particular programming problems.

Style and documentation

Write clear programs that are well laid out with consistent indentation.

Document your program by including appropriate comments.

Write an evaluation describing how well the specification has been met and identify possible improvements.

Errors and testing

Have knowledge about the different types of error that are likely to occur, and be able to interpret error messages and correct the errors.

Be able to describe the importance of testing and know of some techniques for testing your programs. Apply at least one of these to test your programs.

Chapter 1 (Week 1)

1.1 Preliminary knowledge and skills

Whenever any one starts a new course of study, the teacher needs to make some assumptions. It is usually assumed that everyone has used a computer before, but may never have programmed.

I am assuming that you have never programmed before, but have had some acquaintance with a computer running Windows. In particular you will need to know how to do the following.

1. Switch on your computer. If you are in a college environment, you will be given a username and password to logon.

2. Open and close windows

3. Resize and move windows

4. Know how to use an editor such as notepad

5. Be able to create objects such as folders and shortcuts

6. Know how to use a word-processor such as Microsoft Word

7. Have a very basic knowledge of how to access the internet

8. Obtain a screen dump using Print Screen key

9. Be able to use Windows utilities such as Microsoft Paint

In addition to these you will be expected to learn new skills. In particular you will need to learn how to use a particular programming environment, to write and run C++ programs.

This book uses Quincy 2005. This is an **Integrated Development Environment** (IDE) for C++. In simple terms this is a complete package for developing C++ programs. It contains an **editor**, to enable you type in your program. This has the usual facilities that you would expect in an editor such as notepad. So for instance you can save the program, print it, do a cut-and-paste etc. It contains a **compiler** to translate your program into **executable machine code**, and a **debugger** to help you find out what is wrong with your program. There are also a number of other facilities that won't be used in this book.

1.2 What is C++

C++ is still one of the most popular programming languages in the world. Its dominance in the universities has now taken second place to Java, but when it comes to real world programming, there is still an enormous demand for both C and C++ programmers.

C++ is a high-level programming language based on the C language. Like C you can write programs in a **procedural** style. That is, your program is based on a procedure, or sequence of instructions, executed one at a time to perform a desired result.

You can also write **object-oriented** programs. **Object-oriented** programming involves the use of user-defined **classes** and **objects**. A class is a special type of structure or template that defines the properties of an object. It collects together a number of data items, and a number of methods (commonly referred to as member functions) that can act on this data. Once a class has been defined, you can use it as if it is a new data type.

More recently there has been much more extensive use of **templates** – many have now been included in the **standard template library** (STL). Programming using templates and the STL is often referred to as **generic** programming.

This makes C++ a hybrid or multi-paradigm language. That is you can write programs using any of the paradigms previously mentioned. This makes C++ a very flexible and powerful language.

C++ has many similarities in common with C and Java. The syntax for control structures, arrays, arithmetic operators etc are almost identical.

C++ is an extremely large language. Any book that covers it in a fairly comprehensive manner is likely to be large. This book is small, and only covers a small fraction of the topics – only enough to be useful in writing simple programs.

The **standard library** is a massive extension to the C++ language. It is made up of an enormous number of functions, constants and other facilities to support the C++ language. You gain access to parts of the **standard library** by means of **header files**. These header files contain prototypes of functions contained in the standard library. To use one of these header files and gain access to certain functions you use a #include directive.

A common example is

```
#include <iostream>
```

This will be used for virtually every program that you write, as it enables you access to the stream operators, enabling you to use input and output in your program.

This book follows the new ANSI standard. This standard effects both the C++ language and the standard library for C++. This arrived in 1998 and was an attempt to standardise the language. In particular, an important aim was to make sure that if you wrote programs using this standard, they would work on any computer platform. That is they will run with Microsoft Windows, Unix, Linux etc.

You can easily spot a program that does not use this standard, as the header files all have file extensions .h, so for instance you will have **#include <iostream.h>** instead of the statement **#include <iostream>**. Also you will see no reference to **namespaces**. For this reason it is best to use books that are written after 1998. Even still you still need to check out the book first, as there are quite a number of books written after this date that still use the old style.

1.3 A first attempt at programming in C++

For the first programs, we look at simple output. C++ uses streams for input and output. A **stream** is merely a sequence of characters stored in memory.

1.3.1 First version

Example1

```
#include <iostream>

int main()
{
    std::cout << "Hello " << std::endl;

    return 0;
}
```

Notes:

1. The necessary definitions to perform stream input and output are contained within the header file **iostream**. The **#include** directive instructs the compiler to include these definitions in the program.

2. Every C++ program has a **function** called **main()**. Execution of the program starts with the function main().

3. The curly brackets { and } are used to group together program statements. The group of statements is called a **program block**.

4. The **cout** object together with the << operator, is used to output to the screen – in this case the literal string "Hello ".

5. The new-line character **endl** moves the cursor to a new line. If anything else were to be output, it would appear on the next line.

6. Both **cout** and **endl** appear in the namespace **std**. That is they are in the standard C++ library. The **scope resolution operator** :: is needed to indicate that both **cout** and **endl** are in the namespace **std**.

7. The statements `std::cout << "Hello " << std::endl;` and `return 0;` are indented to indicate clearly that they are within the `main()` function. **Indentation** is typically achieved by pressing the tab key, and is an essential feature of programming style used to make the program more readable.

8. An alternative to **endl** is the literal '**\n**'. This is much more familiar to C programmers.

9. The function `main()` should have a return value of type **int**.

10. A return value of 0 in the function `main()`, indicates the program has run successfully.

11. All statements end with a semi-colon.

1.3.2 Second version

Example 2

```
#include <iostream>
using std::cout;
using std::endl;

int main()
{
    cout << "Hello" << endl;

    return 0;
}
```

Notes:

1. The statement **using std::cout;** indicates that every time **cout** is used, it is the **cout** defined in **namespace std**.

2. This is preferable to the first program, as it only has to be done once.

1.3.3   Third version

<u>Example 3</u>

```cpp
#include <iostream>
using namespace std;

int main()
{
    cout << "Hello" << endl;

    return 0;
}
```

Notes:

1. In this version the statement **using namespace std;** is used. This is the most concise program. Use of this statement effectively says that all commands used, are those in the **standard library**.

2. Experienced programmers often scorn this practice, as it can cause problems especially if you are writing large programs that use facilities from libraries other than the standard library. The reason for this is, that there may be functions or constants in these third party libraries that have the same names as those in the standard library. There is then an increased likelihood of ambiguity.

3. The examples in this book only use facilities in the standard library, so there is no danger of this.

1.4 Using the Quincy 2005 IDE

When you load the Quincy IDE, you are given a blank window with 8 pop-down menus at the top. You obtain the following by clicking on **File**.

To create a new C++ program you need to click on **New** from the File pop-down menu. Then click on **C++ source file**. You are then given a blank screen onto which you can type your program.

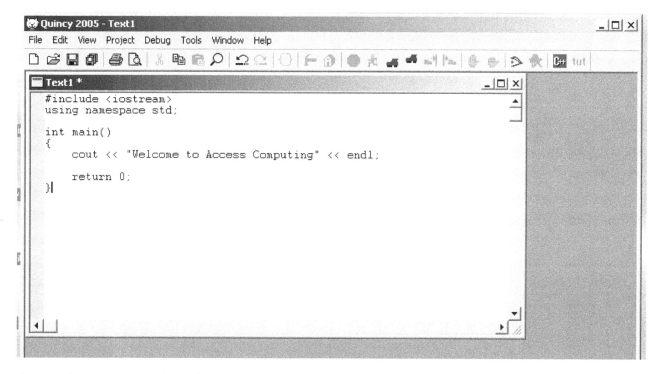

Once the program has been typed in, it is important to save it. The first time you save a program use the **Save As** option. Then periodically use the **Save** option there after.

Once the program has been saved, you will notice that different parts of the program are colour-coded. So for instance all comments may be green, all string literals are red and all keywords are blue etc. This colour-coding does help you spot errors much easier, even before you compile the program.

The previous program was saved as program1. You now need to **compile** the program. The process of compilation translates the **source code** you typed in into another language – in this case machine code (**object code**).

You now need to click on **Build**. This automatically links the included header files and their associated libraries to the object code, and creates executable machine code. In this case, an **exe** file is created with the executable machine code in it. This process is often referred to as **linking**, as the program concerned, links all the necessary header files and libraries into your program. The program itself is called a **linker**. If you are successful, you will get the message "**Successful build**" in both cases.

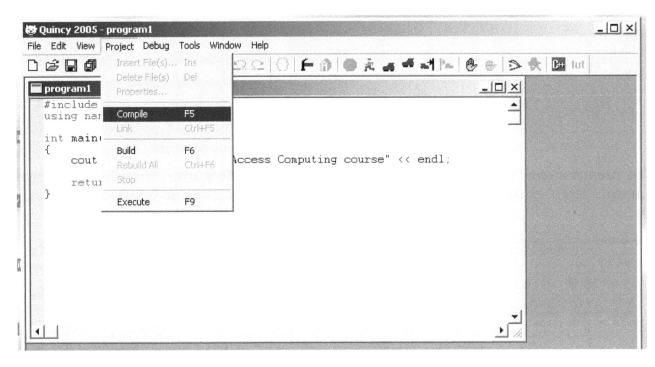

To run the program, click on **Execute** from the **Project** menu or **Run** from the **Debug** menu.

To exit from this console window, you press the Return / Enter key as stated.

It is a good idea to customise the editor for your own needs.

First click on **Tools**, then **Options** and finally the **Editor** tab.

You then obtain the following.

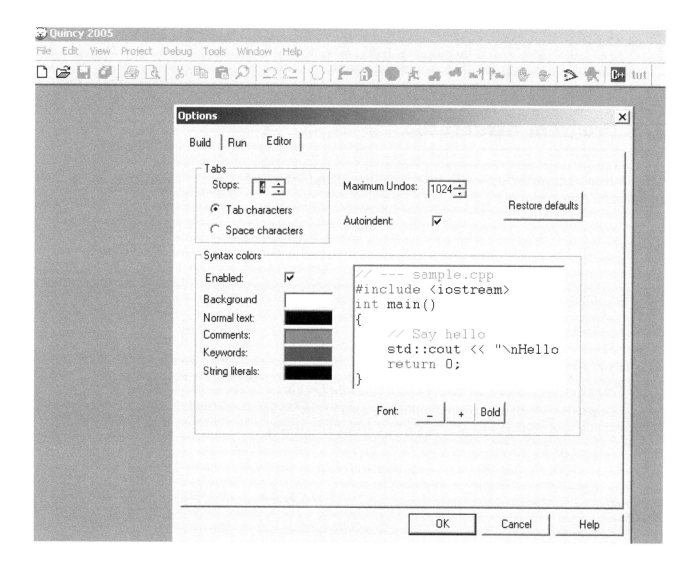

Notes:

1. You can colour code various parts of your program, with a colour of your choice.

2. You can adjust the size of program text by clicking on either – or +.

3. You can adjust the size of the tab (For most purposes 4 is fine).

Exercise 1-1

1. Type in, compile and run the previous programs.

2. Produce a listing for each program, together with a screen dump demonstrating that the program works. Also try cropping the screen dump using Paint.

3. Write a program that will output your name and address. Run this program.

4. Modify the editor settings. Adjust the colour for various aspects of the program. Also, adjust the size of the text.

1.5 Program Structure

The following program will be used to illustrate the basic structure of a C++ program. Also refer to 1.3.1

Example 4

```cpp
#include <iostream>
using namespace std;

int main()
{
    // A first program
    cout << "This is the first line";
    cout << "of my program" << endl;
    cout << "and this is the second line";
    return 0;
}
```

Notes:

1. The symbol // indicates the beginning of a **comment**. A comment is ignored by the compiler. It is only there to be read by the programmer. It is also an important way of documenting the program.

2. The statement **using namespace std;** is used to indicate that all functions used are part of the **standard library**. This is to avoid ambiguity.

3. Every C++ program has at least one function. The one called **main()** is the part of the program that starts running first.

4. **cout** stands for character output. The object **cout** together with the extraction operator << is used to display characters on the screen.

5. To perform character output it is necessary to include the header file **iostream.**

10

6. Each C++ program will contain a function called **main()**. This function will return an integer that determines whether the program was successful or not. A return value of 0 denotes a success.

1.6 Keyboard input

<u>Example 5</u>

```
#include <iostream>
using namespace std;

int main()
{
    // This is my second example program.
    // It demonstrates adding two whole numbers

    int n1, n2, n3;
    cout << "Enter first number ";
    cin >> n1;
    cout << "Enter second number ";
    cin >> n2;
    n3 = n1 + n2;
    cout << "The sum of these numbers is " << n3;

    return 0;
}
```

Notes:

1. The declaration int n1, n2, n3; creates 3 variables for storing integers.

2. A variable is merely a chunk of storage in memory with a name that references the storage. The storage is two bytes for an int.

3. The statement cout << "Enter first number "; is a prompt to the user, telling them to type in a number.

4. The statement cin >> n1; takes whatever input is typed in at the keyboard and stores it in the variable n1.

5. The stream object **cin** is always used with the insertion operator **>>**.

6. The statement n3 = n1 + n2; is called an assignment statement. The contents of variables n1 and n2 are added together and the result is stored in n3.

7. cout << n3; displays the contents of n3.

1.7 Scope

The **scope** of a variable is those parts of the program with which it is accessible. The following program illustrates this concept.

```cpp
#include <iostream>
using namespace std;

int x = 3, y = 5;    //global variables

int main()
{
    cout << "Output from part (1) of the program " << endl;
    cout << "x = " << x << " y = " << y << endl; //(1)

    int a = 4, y = 7;
    cout << "Output from part (2) of the program " << endl;
    cout << "a = " << a << " x = " << x
         << " y = " << y << endl;                           //(2)

    {
        int b = 11, y = 6;
        cout << "Output from part (3) of the program " << endl;
        cout << "a = " << a << " b = " << b
             << " x = " << x << " y = " << y << endl;//(3)
    }

    cout << "Output from part (4) of the program " << endl;
    cout << "a = " << a << " x = " << x
         << " y = " << y << endl;                           //(4)

    return 0;
}
```

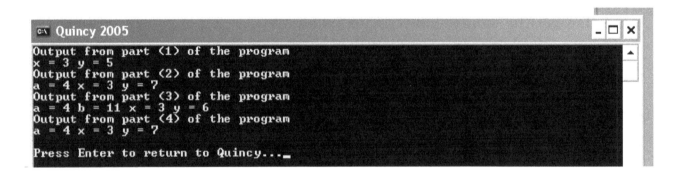

Notes:

In part (1) no variables have been declared at this stage, so the values of the variables at the top of the program are used. These are called **global variables** as they can be accessed from anywhere in the program. We can also say that these variables have **global scope**.

12

In part (2) two new variables have been declared. Even though one of them y has the same name as the **global** variable called y, they are in fact different variables. We can say that y is **local** to the function `main()` or that the scope of this variable is the function `main()`. So when it comes to outputting the value of variables, if a **local** version exists, the value of this variable is used, otherwise the **global** version is used.

In part 3 a **program block** has been created. If a new variable is declared here, the **scope** of the variable is the **program block** itself. That is the **scope** is anywhere between the curly brackets. If a local variable can't be found, but there is a version within main(), then this will be used. If there is no variable with this in main(), then the global variables will be used.

Finally, in part 4, the output statements are outside the program block, and back into the `main()` function. So, you wouldn't be surprised to know that the scope of the variable a is the function `main()`. Because y has not been declared in `main()`, the global variable called y is used.

1.8 Special characters

Example 6

```
#include <iostream>
using namespace std;
int main()
{
    cout << "Demonstration\nof the\nnewline character.\n\n";
    cout << "Demonstrate horizontal tab:\t1\t2\t3" << endl;
    cout << "Demonstrate carriage return\r";
    cout << "Demonstrate bell\a";

    return 0;
}
```

```
Quincy 2005                                                    _|□|×|
Demonstration
of the
newline character.

Demonstrate horizontal tab:      1        2        3
Demonstrate belliage return
Press Enter to return to Quincy..._
```

Escape sequence	Description
\n	Newline. Cursor moves to the next line.
\t	Horizontal tab. Cursor moves to the next tab stop.
\r	Carriage return. Move cursor to the beginning of the current line.
\a	Alert. Make a beeping sound.
\\	Display a backslash (\).
\"	Display a double-quote (").
\?	Display a question mark(?).

1.9 Use of the string class

Example 7

```cpp
#include <iostream>
#include <string>

using namespace std;

int main()
{
    string name;
    cout << "Enter your name: ";
    cin >> name;

    string s = "Hello " + name;
    cout << s;

    return 0;
}
```

```
Quincy 2005                                          _ □ ×
Enter your name: Tony Hawken
Hello Tony
Press Enter to return to Quincy..._
```

Notes:

1. The **string class** is defined in the header file **<string>**. To create string objects you need to include this class.

2. **string name;** creates an object called name that is of type **string**. This string object is initially empty.

3. **cin >> name;** is used to input a string to the object called name. The input is terminated as soon as a **space**, a **tab** or a **Return** is encountered.

4. The + operator when used with a string has a different meaning to that used with numbers. It is used to join two strings together. This is referred to as **concatenation**.

5. **string s = "Hello " + name;** creates a string object called s. It then joins together the literal string "**Hello** " with the contents of the string object called **name**, and stores this in **s**.

6. **cout << s;** is used to display the contents of **s** onto the screen.

1.10 Another example that uses the string class

<u>Example 8</u>

```
#include <iostream>
#include <string>
using namespace std;

int main()
{
    string mystring = "Welcome to the Access Computing course";
    string s1, s2, s3, s4;
    int n;

    n = mystring.length();
    cout << "The string mystring has "
        << n << " characters" << endl;

    s1 = mystring.substr(15, 6);
    cout << "s1 contains " << s1 << endl;

    n = mystring.find("Computing");
    s2 = mystring.substr(n);
    cout << "The word computing is found at position "
        << n << endl;
    s3 = mystring.substr(n);
    cout << "The remaining string after position ";
    cout << n << " is " << s3 << endl;

    return 0;
```

```
}
```

```
Quincy 2005                                                    _ □ ×
The string mystring has 38 characters
s1 contains Access
The word computing is found at position 22
The remaining string after position 22 is Computing course

Press Enter to return to Quincy..._
```

Notes:

1. Strings can be initialised at the time they are created. The string mystring is initialised with the value "Welcome to the Access Computing course"

2. The string function **length()** returns the length of the string object calling the function.

3. The function call **substr(x, n);** returns the string starting at position x with the next n characters.

4. The function call **mystring.find("Computing");** locates the position of the first character of the word "Computing" in the string mystring.

5. The function call **mystring.substr(n);** returns the end of the string mystring, starting with position n.

1.11   Use of getline() for input of strings

Example 9

```
#include <iostream>
#include <string>
using namespace std;

int main()
{
    string name, addr1, addr2, postcode;
    // Enter name and address
    cout << "Enter your name\t\t";
    getline(cin, name);
    cout << "First line of address\t";
    getline(cin, addr1);
    cout << "Second line of address\t";
    getline(cin, addr2);
    cout << "Postcode\t\t";
    getline(cin, postcode);

    // Display name and address
    cout << name << endl;
```

```
        cout << addr1 << endl;
        cout << addr2 << endl;
        cout << postcode;
        return 0;
}
```

```
Quincy 2005                                                    _ □ ×
Enter your name           Fred Bloggs
First line of address     249 any road
Second line of address    anytown
Postcode                  AB45 5AE
Fred Bloggs
249 any road
anytown
AB45 5AE
Press Enter to return to Quincy...
```

Notes:

1. The insertion operator >> cannot be used to input a line of an address because all white-space (spaces and tabs) are interpreted as separators of data items. When a space is detected, this is interpreted as the end of the data being read.

2. The function getline() can be used to read an entire line of text. Spaces are not interpreted as special characters.

3. The character \t is used to move to the next tab position. This is especially useful if you want to line up your output.

1.12   Correcting Errors

1.12.1   Syntax errors

A syntax error, is a mistake in grammar. This usually involves a misspelling or expressing a statement in an incorrect format. The following illustrates one of the most common errors. This is also called a compile-time error, as it is detected by the compiler during compilation.

Example 10

```
#include <iostream>
using namespace std;

int main()
{
     cout << "Hello, are you there? " << endl
}
```

When you compile the program, you obtain the following.

```
Build                                                                    ☒
"C:\Program Files\quincy\mingw\bin\gcc.exe" -fno-rtti -fno-exceptions -std=c++98 -pedantic-error
d:\course\access computing\unit2\prog\compile1.cpp: In function 'int main()':
d:\course\access computing\unit2\prog\compile1.cpp:7: error: expected `;' before '}' token
Unsuccessful build
```

From this, you can obtain the following information.

```
Compile1.cpp: In function 'int main()'.
Compile1.cpp:7 : error : expected ';' before '}' token
Unsuccessful build
```

More specifically there is a missing semicolon after `endl`.

1.12.2   Other compile-time errors

The following program illustrates another very common mistake.

Example 11

```
#include <iostream>
using namespace std;

int main()
{
     string word;
     cout >> "Enter the next word";
     cin << word;
```

```
        return 0;
}
```

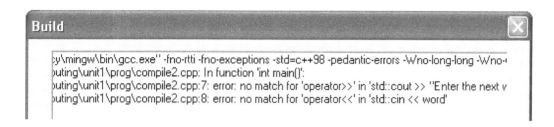

From this you can obtain the following information.

```
compile2.cpp : In function 'int main()'
compile2.cpp : 7 : error : no match for 'operator >>' in
'std::cout >> "Enter next word"'
compile2.cpp : 8 : error : no match for 'operator <<' in 'std::cin
<< word'
```

If you haven't spotted exactly what the error is, it is to do with the operators associated with `cin` and `cout`.

1.12.3   Link-time errors

This looks like a compiler error because it was detected by the compiler, but it was not due to any mistake, other than the fact that the program is incomplete. The precompiler directive #include <iostream> is missing.

Example 12

```
int main()
{
        std::cout << "Welcome to Access computing" << std::endl;
        return 0;
}
```

Build

```
"C:\Program Files\quincy\mingw\bin\gcc.exe" -fno-rtti -fno-exceptions -std=c++98 -pedantic-error
d:\course\access computing\unit1\prog\link.cpp: In function 'int main()':
d:\course\access computing\unit1\prog\link.cpp:3: error: 'cout' is not a member of 'std'
d:\course\access computing\unit1\prog\link.cpp:3: error: 'endl' is not a member of 'std'
Unsuccessful build
```

From this you can obtain the following information.

```
link.cpp: in 'int function main()'
link.cpp: 3: error: 'cout' is not a member of 'std'
link.cpp: 3: error 'endl' is not a member of 'std'
```

The reason the compiler says that cout and endl is not a member of std, is the fact that this information is contained in the header file <iostream>.

1.11.4   Run-time errors

A run-time error occurs when you run the program. Not all run-time errors result in error messages. In this example, the program appears to run correctly, but it is obvious that one of the results is incorrect.

Example 13

```cpp
#include <iostream>
using namespace std;

int main()
{
    int n = 1000;
    cout << "n = " << n << endl;
    n *= n;
    cout << "n = " << n << endl;
    n *= n;
    cout << "n = " << n << endl;

    return 0;
}
```

```
Quincy 2005
n = 1000
n = 1000000
n = -727379968

Press Enter to return to Quincy..._
```

This error occurred due to the fact that the size of the calculated value of n exceeded the maximum size of an int. This type of error is called **integer overflow**. In this particular example, there was overflow into the sign bit, causing the number to become negative.

1.11.5   Another run-time example

This example includes an error code in the output.

Example 14

```cpp
#include <iostream>
using namespace std;

int main()
{
    float a = 15.75, b = 3.0;
    cout << (a/b) << endl;
    cout << (a / (b - 3.0)) << endl;

    return 0;
```

20

}

The error is caused because there is a division by zero. This example is extremely contrived. This type of error will often be much more subtle. The INF denotes infinity. If you to perform this type of calculation on a calculator you will typically obtain the error message "Math ERROR".

There will be cases when the program compiles, runs and gives some output that does not contain an error message. The problem is, is that the output is wrong. There is a problem with the program logic. This is often referred to as a **logic error**.

Exercise 1-2

1. Fill in the blanks for the following program

```
#include _____
#include _____
using _____
int _____ ()

_____
        string guest;
        cout _____ "Enter name for first guest ";
        cin _____ guest;
        guest = "Mr " + guest;
        cout _____ "Hello " _____ guest _____ _____ ;
        return_____ ;
}
```

2. Each of the following programs has one or more errors. Locate the error. Identify the type of error and then correct the program.

    (a)   ```
            #include <iostream>
            using namespace std;
            int main()
            {
                int n += 22;
                cout << n << endl;
            }
            ```
            ```

```
(b)    #include <iostream>
       using namespace std;
       int main(void)
       {
              string name;
              cout "Enter full name";
              cin >> name;
              name = "Mr " + name;
              cout << "Hello " + name;

              return 0;
       }

(c)    #include <iostream
       int main()
       {
              std::cout << "Enter 2 numbers " << endl;
              cin >> n1 >> n2;
              n3 = n1 + n2;
              std::cout << "sum = " n3 << endl;

              return 0;
       }
```

3. Write a program that will store your full name in a string. The program will then output your names in reverse order with a comma separating the names.

For example if input string is: Tony Hawken
The required output is: Hawken, Tony

Chapter 2 (Week 2)

2.1 Primitive data types

All data is stored in **binary** (base 2) format. That is it is represented as a sequence of zeros and ones. Any one of these ones or zeros is referred to as a **binary digit** or **bit**. Normally these bits are packaged together into a unit of storage called a **byte**. Here 1 byte = 8 bits.

The following data types are standard in C++

integers	int, short int, long int (can be signed or unsigned)
real numbers	float, double, long double
characters	char (can be signed or unsigned), wchar_t
wide characters	wchar_t (used to store unicode characters)
boolean	bool (true or false)

A **char** is considered to be a very small number, as it takes up only 1 byte of storage. Each character is represented by a number – the **ASCII code** of that character. You can store a **char** using a number (its ASCII code) or the character itself.

An integer is a whole number. They can be negative or positive. The keywords **short** and **long** are data type modifiers. An **int** usually takes up two bytes of storage, wheras **long int**, typically takes up 4 bytes of storage.

Both **floats** and **double** are used to store floating point numbers. These are used to represent real numbers. In computing terms a real number is merely a number that needs a decimal point in it. This would be called a rational number in mathematics. The double type has a greater precision than that of a float. That is you can represent a number with many more numbers after the decimal point.

2.2 Variable declaration

- All variables need to be declared before they are used.

- When a variable is declared, storage is allocated to store data.

- A variable name cannot be a C++ keyword (reserved word)

Example statements

```
int x, y, z, sum;
char ans;
float average;
bool success;
```

2.3 Variable assignment

- Assignment is used to store data in a variable

- The **assignment** operator is denoted by **=**

Example statements

```
x = 3; y = 2; z = 5;
ans = 'y';
ans = 64;
average = (x + y + z)/ 3.0;
success = true;
int a = 5;
const double pi = 3.14159;
```

Notes:

1. `x = 3;` stores the value 3 in the variable called x.

2. `ans = 'y';` stores the character constant y. Note single quotes are required for character constants.

3. `ans = 64;` Stores the character with ASCII code 64.

4. `average = (x + y + z) / 3.0;` Computes RHS and stores the result in average. Need to use 3.0 rather than 3 for floating-point division.

5. The keyword **const**, indicates that the variable cannot be modified. That is, you have created a constant.

2.4 C++ keywords

The following are reserved words in both the C and C++ languages. They cannot be used for variable names:

auto	break	case	char	const	continue
default	do	double	else	enum	extern
float	for	goto	if	int	long
register	return	short	signed	sizeof	static
struct	switch	typedef	union	unsigned	void
volatile	while				

The following are C++ only keywords:

asm	bool	catch	class	const_cast	delete
dynamic_cast	explicit	false	friend	inline	mutable
namespace	new	operator	private	protected	public
reinterpret_cast		static_cast	template	this	throw
true	try	typeid	typename	using	virtual
wchar_t					

In addition to these there are alternative representations for operators. These also are reserved and should not be used otherwise.

and	&&	and_eq	&=	bitand	&	bitor	|
compl	~	not	!	not_eq	!=	or	||
or_eq	|=	xor	^	xor_eq	^=		

You may want to refer back to this list from time to time, so that you can tick off those keywords with which you are familiar.

2.5 Arithmetic operators

2.5.1   Integer operators

The following arithmetic operations are called **binary operators** as they are used to combine two numbers. Each calculation with these operators should result in an integer when integer operands are used:

operator	description	example
+	add	a + b
-	subtract	a - b
-	negate	-a
*	multiply	a * b;
/	divide	a / b
%	remainder	a % b

The following program demonstrates the use of arithmetic operators:

Example 15

```cpp
#include <iostream>
using namespace std;

int main()
{
    int a, b;
    cout << "Enter two integers: ";
    cin >> a >> b;

    cout << "Sum = " << (a + b) << endl;

    cout << "Difference = " << (a - b) << endl;

    cout << "Product = " << (a * b) << endl;

    cout << "Quotient = " << (a / b) << endl;

    cout << "remainder = " << (a % b) << endl;

    return 0;
}
```

```
Quincy 2005                                          _ □ ×
Enter two integers: 11 4
Sum = 15
Difference = 7
Product = 44
Quotient = 2
remainder = 3

Press Enter to return to Quincy...
```

Notes

1. The expression a + b is contained within brackets to force the expression to be evaluated, before it is displayed using `cout`. This would be unnecessary if we were using assignment.

2. Integer division loses the remainder. So 11 / 4 gives the result 2, not 2.75.

The following program demonstrates integer division and the remainder operator:

Example 16

```cpp
#include <iostream>
using namespace std;

int main()
{
    int cm;
    cout << "Enter a distance in cm : ";
    cin >> cm;

    int km = cm / 100000;      // integer division - extract km
    cm = cm % 100000;    // save remainder after extracting km
    int m = cm / 100;     // integer division - extract m
    cm = cm % 100;        // save remainder - leaves cm left over

    // Output resuts
    cout << "Number of km : " << km << endl;
    cout << "Number of m  : " << m << endl;
    cout << "Number of cm : " << cm << endl;

    return 0;
}
```

Notes:

1. The result of the division given by **km = cm / 100000;** will be an integer, because both cm and 100000 are integers.

2. The statement **cm = cm % 100000;** will divide the current value of cm by 100000 and store the remainder in cm.

27

Arithmetic operators are normally used with an assignment operator. An assignment statement is a bit like a formula in mathematics. On the right-hand-side of the = sign, you have a calculation to work out. The result is then stored in the variable on the left-hand-side.

You could take the formula $E = mc^2$

Which can be interpreted as $E = m \times c^2$ or $E = m \times c \times c$

Written as a C++ statement, this becomes

E = m * c * c;

With a statement like this, the computer will work out the product of $m \times c \times c$ and then store the result in E.

2.5.2   Assignment, increment and decrement operators

There are a number of assignment operators besides the most used =. For instance, if you want to add 10 to the current value of a variable you could use either of the following statements.

x = x + 10;

is equivalent to

x += 10;

The following is a list of the other assignment operators.

+=   -=   *=   /=   %=

More will be said about these later, when we have a use for them

In addition both C and C++ have increment and decrement operators. These work on a single integer value.

Operator	description	example		
++	increment	++a	or	a++
--	decrement	--a	or	a--

The statement   x++;

is merely a shorthand for the statement   x = x + 1;
or   x += 1;

That is, add one to the current value of x, then store this new value in x.

2.5.3   The data-types float and double

The data-types float and double are both used to represent numbers that have a fractional part. The data-type double is to be preferred where greater precision is required.

Example 17 (Simple example using float)

```cpp
#include <iostream>
using namespace std;

int main()
{
    float c, f;
    cout << "Program to compute Fahrenheit given centigrade"
        << endl;
    c = 24;
    f = c * 9/5 + 32;
    cout << "The temperature " << c << " centigrade is " << f;

    cout << " degrees Fahrenheit" << endl;
    return 0;
}
```

```
Quincy 2005                                                    _ □ ×
Program to compute Fahrenheit given centigrade
The temperature 24 centigrade is 75.2 degrees Fahrenheit

Press Enter to return to Quincy..._
```

Notes:

1. At least one of the operands on the right-hand-side of the assignment operator must be a float to perform floating-point division. Otherwise the result will be treated as an integer before storing as a float.

2. You can convert an integer to a float simply by adding a decimal point. That is 5.0 is a float, but 5 is considered to be an int.

3. The evaluation of `c * 9/5 + 32` is determined by precedence, the same as working out a mathematical expression. That is, brackets, multiply or divide, then add or subtract.

4. Operators with equal precedence are evaluated left-to-right. That is the main arithmetic operators are left-to-right associative.

5. There are 18 levels of precedence in C++. We won't complicate things by mentioning this further.

Another similar example follows:

Example 18

```cpp
#include <iostream>
using namespace std;

int main()
{
    float a, b, c, d, e, av;
    cout << "Enter 5 numbers : ";
    cin >> a >> b >> c >> d >> e;
    av = (a + b + c + d + e) / 5.0;
    cout << "Average is " << av << endl;
    return 0;
}
```

```
C:\ Quincy 2005                                          _ □ ×
Enter 5 numbers : 3 5 7 8 9
Average is 6.4

Press Enter to return to Quincy...
```

Notes:

1. The statement cin >> a >> b >> c >> d >> e; is used to input 5 floats into the variables a, b, c, d, and e.

2. White space needs to separate each of these numbers. This can be a single space, multiple spaces, or a carriage return.

3. To obtain the correct value for **av** it is necessary to divide by 5.0, not 5.

Example 19 (demonstrate integer and real division)

```cpp
#include <iostream>
using namespace std;

int main()
{
    cout << 22 / 5 << endl;        // integer division
    cout << 22.0 / 5.0 << endl;    // Real division
    return 0;
}
```

```
C:\ Quincy 2005                                          _ □ ×
4
4.4

Press Enter to return to Quincy..._
```

Notes:

1. C++ style comments can be added to programs by placing // before the comment. Anything after // for the rest of the line is ignored by the compiler.

2. A division involving integers will give an integer result.

3. A division involving floats will give a float as the result. At least one of the operand must be a float for a floating-point division to take place.

2.5.4 Standard form

Standard form is used to represent either very large numbers, or very small numbers. The following program illustrates how to represent numbers using standard form in a C++ program.

Standard form is based on powers of 10. As a reminder I will include some powers of 10.

$10^2 = 10 \times 10 = 100$, $10^3 = 10 \times 10 \times 10 = 1000$ and so on.

If you take a number such as 312000 you can write it as a number times a power of 10. $312000 = 3.12 \times 100000 = 3.2 \times 10^5$.

It is this last number that is said to be in standard form or uses scientific notation.

<u>Example 20</u> (Use standard form to represent floating point numbers)

```cpp
#include <iostream>
using namespace std;

int main()
{
    double x = 5.89e-6;
    double y = 100000.0;

    cout << (x * y) << endl;

    return 0;
}
```

```
Quincy 2005                                    _ □ ×
0.589
Press Enter to return to Quincy...■
```

Notes:

1. 5.89e-6 is equivalent to 5.89×10^{-6}

31

2.6 Determine storage required for different data types

The size of a variable depends on its type. For most systems the following is typical:

char = 1 byte, short int = 2 bytes, int = 4 bytes, long int = 4 bytes, float = 4 bytes, double = 8 bytes, long double = 10 or 12 bytes.

The exact value is system dependent. To determine how much storage is required on yours system – that is using Quincy 2005 (or your chosen IDE/Compiler if you prefer another), the following program has been written.

<u>Example 21</u>

```cpp
// Display size of a variable in bytes using sizeof()
#include <iostream>
using namespace std;

int main()
{
    char a;
    int b;
    float c;
    double d;
    bool e;
    wchar_t f;
    short g;
    long h;
    long double i;

    cout << "Size of a char is " << sizeof(a) << endl;
    cout << "Size of an int is " << sizeof(b) << endl;
    cout << "Size of a float is " << sizeof(c) << endl;
    cout << "Size of a double is " << sizeof(d) << endl;
    cout << "Size of a bool is " << sizeof(e) << endl;
    cout << "Size of wchar_t is " << sizeof(f) << endl;
    cout << "Size of short is " << sizeof(g) << endl;
    cout << "Size of long is " << sizeof(h) << endl;
    cout << "Size of long double is " << sizeof(i);

    return 0;
}
```

```
Quincy 2005
Size of a char is 1
Size of an int is 4
Size of a float is 4
Size of a double is 8
Size of a bool is 1
Size of wchar_t is 2
Size of short is 2
Size of long is 4
Size of long double is 12
Press Enter to return to Quincy..._
```

Notes:

1. The `sizeof()` operator is used to determine the size in bytes of any of the primitive data types.

2. The size of various integer data types can also be determined by using the header <climits>.

3. The constants CHAR_MIN, SHRT_MIN, INT_MIN, LONG_MIN contain values of the minimum possible value of a char, short, int, and long respectively.

4. The constants CHAR_MAX, SHRT_MAX, INT_MAX, LONG_MAX contain values of the maximum possible value of a char, short, int, and long respectively.

The following illustrates these constants:

Example 22

```cpp
#include <iostream>
#include <climits>

using namespace std;

int main()
{
    cout << "Minimum Vales" << endl;
    cout << "Smallest value of a char is " << CHAR_MIN << endl;
    cout << "Smallest value of a short is " << SHRT_MIN << endl;
    cout << "Smallest value of a int is " << INT_MIN << endl;
    cout << "Smallest value of a long is " << LONG_MIN << endl;

    cout << "Maximum values" << endl;
    cout << "Largest value of a char is " << CHAR_MAX << endl;
    cout << "Largest value of a short is " << SHRT_MAX << endl;
    cout << "Largest value of a int is " << INT_MAX << endl;
    cout << "Largest value of a long is " << LONG_MAX << endl;

    return 0;
}
```

```
Quincy 2005                                                    _ □ ✕
Minimum Vales
Smallest value of a char is -128
Smallest value of a short is -32768
Smallest value of a int is -2147483648
Smallest value of a long is -2147483648
Maximum values
Largest value of a char is 127
Largest value of a short is 32767
Largest value of a int is 2147483647
Largest value of a long is 2147483647

Press Enter to return to Quincy...
```

Exercise 2-1

1. Fill in the following table to show the current state of each variable as each line of code executes:

Code	x	y	z
`int x = 0;`			
`double y, z = 3.0;`			
`y = 0.6 * z;`			
`x = 0.4 * z;`			
`x = 12;`			
`y = 3;`			
`z = x / y;`			
`x++;`			
`y = ++x;`			
`z *= 2;`			

2 (a) Write a program that will display the following menu, and prompt a user:-

```
            Menu
            ----
    1.    Play space invaders
    2.    Play PACMAN
    3.    Play Super Mario
    4.    Quit menu

    Enter your choice (1-4) :
```

   (b) Allow the user to enter a number, and then print out their choice

3. The formula :

$$GM = \frac{F - 275}{25} + 1$$

   gives an approximate conversion from degrees Fahrenheit to the British Gas mark on a cooker for temperatures between 275 and 1000 degrees F. Write a short program that will :-

   (a)   allow a user to enter a temperature in Fahrenheit which is between 275 and 1000F.
   (b)   Compute the Gas mark and print out the result in an appropriate format.
   (c)   include appropriate comments to make the program readable.

4. Write a program which given a number representing an ASCII code will print the corresponding character.

5. Einstein's most famous equation is $E = mc^2$. This calculates an amount of energy in Joules given a loss in mass (m) in Kg. It uses the speed of light (c).

   Given that the speed of light is 299,792,500 ms^{-1}, write a program that calculates and prints out E. Represent c as a numeric constant. Choose appropriate data types.

6. Write a program to work out a person's change. It is assumed that the item costs less than £10 and that the person only has a £10 note to pay with. The required change should then be calculated so that a minimum number of coins are given. No notes are given as change.

Analysis of problem (q6)

1. Easier if change is converted to pence.
2. Coins currently available are £2, £1, 50p, 20p, 10p, 5p, 2p, 1p.
3. Need to keep a coin count for each coin.
4. Can use the built-in arithmetic operators / and %.

2.7 Solve quadratic equations

A quadratic equation is an equation of the form $ax^2 + bx + c = 0$

it can be solved with the formula:

$$x = \frac{-b \pm \sqrt{b^2 - 4ac}}{2a}$$

this provides us with two solutions

$$x1 = \frac{-b + \sqrt{b^2 - 4ac}}{2a} \quad \text{and} \quad x2 = \frac{-b - \sqrt{b^2 - 4ac}}{2a}$$

These can be coded as:

```
x1 := (-b + sqrt(b * b - 4 * a * c)) / (2 * a);
x2 := (-b - sqrt(b * b - 4 * a * c)) / (2 * a);
```

You will notice that `sqrt(b * b - 4 * a * c)` is repeated in both assignment statements and so to make the computation more efficient it should be broken down into smaller components.

```
d := sqrt(b * b - 4 * a * c); // only worked out once
x1 := (-b + d) / (2 * a);
x2 := (-b - d) / (2 * a);
```

The complete program will then end up like this:

Example 23

```cpp
#include <iostream>
#include <cmath>
using namespace std;

int main()
{
    float a, b, c, d, x1, x2;
    cout << "Enter coefficients a b c : ";
    cin >> a >> b >> c;
    d = sqrt(b*b - 4*a*c);
    x1 = (-b + d)/(2*a);
    x2 = (-b - d)/(2*a);
    cout << "x is either " << x1 << " or " << x2 << endl;
    return 0;
}
```

```
Quincy 2005                                              _ □ ×
Enter coefficients a b c : 1 -12 16
x is either 10.4721 or 1.52786

Press Enter to return to Quincy...
```

Exercise 2-2

1.   Type in and test the above program. Use it to solve the following equations:

(a) $3x^2 + 7x - 11 = 0$ (b) $x^2 - 12x + 16 = 0$

(c) $4x^2 - 3x + 14 = 0$ (d) $5x^2 - 6x + 35 = 0$

2.8 Use of <iomanip> to format output

The <iomanip> header file allows you to format your output. In the simplest instance you want to be able to specify how many spaces are to be taken up by a number, and how many decimal places you want to display.

<u>Example 24</u>

```
/*    Program to compute area and circumference
      Demonstrates the use of I/O manipulators
      to format floating point numbers               */

#include <iomanip>
#include <iostream>
using namespace std;

int main()
{
      float area, circ, radius;
      const float pi = 3.14159;
      cout << "Enter radius : ";
      cin >> radius;
      area = pi * radius * radius;
      circ = 2 * pi * radius;
       // fixed, setw() and setprecision() require <iomanip>
      cout << fixed << setw(5) << setprecision(2);
      cout << "area = "  << area << endl;
      cout << "circumference = " << circ << endl;
      return 0;
}
```

```
Quincy 2005                                          _ | □ | X |
Enter radius : 4.56
area = 65.33
circumference = 28.66

Press Enter to return to Quincy..._
```

Notes :

1. **iomanip** and **iostream**   are header files that contain definitions required to use certain predefined functions

2. There are two types of comment commonly used in C++

3. // is a C++ style comment. Everything to the right of // is ignored by the compiler

4. /* and */ are used to create C style comments. Everything between these two symbols is ignored by the compiler

5. The keyword **const** is used to show that pi is a constant. The old-fashioned way of doing this, typical of C programmers is: `#define pi 3.14159`

6. **fixed** indicates that the floating point is fixed.

7. The **setw()** function sets the total width of a numeric string.

8. The **setprecision()** function sets the number of digits after the decimal point.

9. If they contain a parameter, the I/O manipulation functions require **<iomanip>** to work.

2.9 Use of <iomanip> to change base

All numbers are stored in binary format. By default when integers are displayed using cout, they are displayed as a base 10 (denary) number. Manipulators available in <iomanip> can be used to change the way numbers are displayed.

Example 25

```
#include <iostream>
#include <iomanip>
using namespace std;

int main()
{
    int x = 123;
    cout << "Decimal number = " << x << endl;
    cout << "Octal number = " << oct << x << endl;
    cout << "Hexadecimal number = " << hex << x << endl;

    return 0;
}
```

```
Quincy 2005                                                  _ |□| ×|
Decimal number = 123
Octal number = 173
Hexadecimal number = 7b

Press Enter to return to Quincy...
```

Notes:

1. The manipulators **dec**, **oct** and **hex** are used to display numbers in decimal (base 10), octal (base 8) and hexadecimal (base 16) respectively.

2. These operators can also be used with cin.

Exercise 2-3

1. Write a program that will prompt a user for an amount in pounds. The program will then convert this value into euros and display the amount to 2 decimal places.   (Assume that 1 pound = 1.009 euros.)

2. The numbers 3, 4 and 5 are an example of a Pythagorean triple because

   $3^2 + 4^2 = 5^2$ (Pythagoras theorem)
   There is a simple formula that gives all Pythagorean triples. Suppose m and n are two positive integers, with m > n then $m^2 - n^2$, $2mn$ and $m^2 + n^2$ is a Pythagorean triple.

   Write a program that inputs 2 integers and can be used to compute Pythagorean triples

3. Write a program that inputs an octal number and will output the decimal equivalent. You can use the following test data. The octal number 214 should give 140 decimal.

Chapter 3 (week 3)

3.1 Boolean expressions

A **boolean** (logical) expression always evaluates to **true** or **false**. When programming decisions and repetitions are used we often need the following operators:

Operator	Meaning	Additions for new standard
<	< (less than)	
>	> (greater than)	
<=	≤ (less than or equal)	
>=	≥ (greater than or equal)	
==	= (equal to)	
!=	≠ (not equal to)	
&&	**Logical and**	operator keyword **and**
||	**Logical or**	operator keyword **or**
!	**not**	operator keyword **not**

The operators <, >, <=, >=, ==, != are known as relational operators. They are used to form a comparison between two numbers or in the new standard – two strings.

A comparison such as:

a < b   will evaluate to **true** or **false**

Should you have problems working out the truth values of logical expressions, you can always check by printing them out.

```
cout << ( a < b);        should display 1 or 0.
```

Here 1 is to be interpreted as true, and 0 as false.

The unary operator **not** is used to negate an expression. That is, an expression whose value is **true** will become **false** and vis versa.

The above expression when negated then becomes:

```
not(a < b)
```

The logical operators **&&** and **||** are used to combine simple logical expressions to form more complex ones. Here is an example.

```
(x > 5)   &&   (x < 20)
```

An expression formed with the **&&** operator like the one above will only evaluate **true** if both of the simpler conditions are **true**. Note that we can use the operator **and** in place of **&&**. In the example above we are testing whether the value of x is in the range 5 and 20.

i.e. 5 < x < 20

The logical operator **||** when used to combine two expressions will evaluate **true** if either or both of the expressions are **true**.

The expression **(x > 5) || (y == 0)** is interpreted as **true** if either of the expressions or both evaluate **true**. Note that the operator **or** can be used in place of **||**.

For your clarification I have included truth tables of the operators **and, or** and **not**.

AND

x	y	x && y
F	F	F
T	F	F
F	T	F
T	T	T

OR

x	y	x ∥ y
F	F	F
T	F	T
F	T	T
T	T	T

NOT

x	! x
F	T
T	F

Truth tables

Example 26

```
#include <iostream>
using namespace std;

int main()
{
        int a = 3, b = 6;
        cout << (a < b);

        return 0;
}
```

Notes:

1. **a < b** is between brackets to force the evaluation of a and b. That is the values of a are used, rather than a and b themselves. This is important if you are going to use the **cout** statement.

2. The resulting output is **1**. A one in this context is interpreted as **true**.

3.2 String comparison

You can also use the relational operators for string comparisons. The order of two characters, is determined by the relative value of their ASCII code. Roughly speaking the purpose of performing String Comparison is to order strings according to alphabetical order. This of course will work provided that only alphabetic characters of the same case are used in the strings.

In the ASCII table we have:

		codes
Numeric characters	0 - 9	48 - 57
Uppercase characters	A - Z	65 - 90
Lowercase characters	a - z	97 - 122

As well as punctuation characters, various non-printing characters and also some graphics characters are present.

So we could write the following valid expressions:

"a" < "b"	Each of these can be verified by checking
"Z" < "a"	an ASCII table.
"4" < "6"	

Two strings are ordered by comparing their characters one at a time until there is a mismatch. Consider the following:

"business" < "busy"

Which can be represented as:

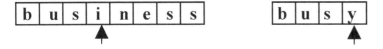

Here the first mismatch is at character position 4 indicating that "business" < "busy". In the same way if we consider the comparison of:

"word" < "words"

This would evaluate true because the first mismatch would be detected on the fifth character, making this expression true. We can also use all of the other relational operators to compare two strings.

Exercise 3-1

1.   Some examples of Boolean (relational) expressions follow

(a)   `5 == 7`   (e)   `(15 > 5) and (7 == 0)`

(b)   `9 <= 9`   (f)   `not(15 > 5) or (7 == 0)`

(c)   `11 > (14 - 5)`   (g)   `not(15 > 5) or (7 = 0)`

(d)   `(15 > 5) or (7 = 0)`   (h)   `not((15 > 5) and (7 = 0))`

For each of the 8 expressions above determine whether they evaluate true or false. You can check your answers by running a C++ statement of the form:

```
cout << ( < Boolean expression > );
```

Note: if you don't want an answer of form 0 or 1, you will also need to use the manipulator boolalpha. This will then give the answer as either true or false. You need to use a statement like this.

```
cout << boolalpha << (<Boolean expression>);
```

For example, the first question could be checked with the following.

```
cout << boolalpha << (5 == 7);
```

3.3 Conditional Statements (The if statement)

We often want the execution of a statement to depend on a condition. This is achieved using a conditional statement such as an **if** statement. Using the terminology of Computer Science, we call this **selection**.

In c++ the simplest format of the **if** statement is:

```
if <boolean expression> then
    <statement>
```

This is to be interpreted as - if the expression is true execute the statement, otherwise do nothing.

e.g.   `if (num > 0 )`
            `cout << "num is positive";`

This can be extended to provide an action if the expression evaluates false.

e.g.   `if num > 0 then`
            `cout << "positive";`
       `else`
            `cout << "non-positive";`

43

Generally speaking the **if ... else** construct as shown above has the following format:

```
if (<boolean expression>)
      <statement 1>;
else
      <statement 2>;
```

which should be interpreted as:

Evaluate the boolean expression. If it is true execute statement 1, otherwise execute statement 2.

This example can be taken a stage further. After all if we are going to classify numbers we might want to say they are Negative, Zero or Positive.

```
if (num < 0 )
      cout << "negative";
else if  (num > 0)
      cout << "positive";
else
      cout << "ZERO";
```

The **else if** enables us to provide another test, and hence another statement to execute if the second expression evaluates true. If neither of the conditions is true then the final statement is executed.

The complete program follows:

Example 27

```
#include <iostream>
using namespace std;

int main()
{
     float num;
     cout << "Enter a number ";
     cin >> num;
     if (num < 0)
          cout << "Number is negative";
     else if (num > 0)
          cout << "Number is positive";
     else
          cout << "Number is zero";
     return 0;
}
```

This is the full format of the **if** statement, often called a multi-way statement. It is an implementation of a construct in Computer Science called the CASE structure. Later on we will see that there is another statement which can be used in many situations where the **if** statement could be used.

The following program performs a range check - in this case that a number is between 1 and 10.

Example 28

```cpp
#include <iostream>
using namespace std;

int main()
{
    int num;
    cout << "Enter a number between 1 and 10 : ";
    cin >> num;
    cout << endl;
    if (num >= 1 and num <= 10)
        cout << "Data correct";
    else
        cout << "Data incorrect";
    return 0;
}
```

```
Enter a number between 1 and 10 : 7

Data correct
Press Enter to return to Quincy..._
```

In the following example, we are comparing the length of a string to see if it is too large. If it is, the string is then truncated

Example 29

```cpp
#include <iostream>
#include <string>
using namespace std;

int main()
{
    string name;
    cout << "Enter name - maximum 10 letters: ";
    cin >> name;
    if (name.length() > 10)
    {
        cerr << "Name entered is too long" << endl;
        cerr << "Truncation will occur" << endl;
        name = name.substr(0, 10);
    }
    cout << "Current value of name = " << name << endl;

    return 0;
}
```

```
Enter name - maximum 10 letters: Encyclopaedia
Name entered is too long
Truncation will occur
Current value of name = Encyclopae

Press Enter to return to Quincy...
```

Notes:

1. In this example **cerr** is used in place of **cout** to display the error message. The object **cerr** is linked to the **standard error stream**. The content of this stream is also sent to the screen. So there appears to be no difference between using cout and cerr.

A common technique to check that a user has not miss-typed their password is to make them enter the same password twice. It can also be used in other situations where it is easy to make a mistake, such as typing in coded data

<u>Example 30</u>

```cpp
#include <iostream>
#include <string>
using namespace std;

int main()
{
    string pwd, pwd1, pwd2;
    cout << "Enter new password ";
    cin >> pwd1;
    cout << "Verification - re-enter password ";
    cin >> pwd2;
    if (pwd1 == pwd2)
    {
        pwd = pwd1;
        cout << "Password successfully changed" << endl;
    }
    else
        cout << "Verifcation failed - password unchanged"
            << endl;

    return 0;
}
```

```
Enter new password ComputerScience
Verification - re-enter password ComputerScience
Password successfully changed

Press Enter to return to Quincy...
```

3.4 Use of a ternary operator

<u>Example 31</u>

```cpp
#include <iostream>
using namespace std;

int main()
{
    int a, b;
    cout << "Enter two integers : ";
    cin >> a >> b;
    cout << "The smallest value is ";
    cout << (a < b ? a : b) << endl;

    return 0;
}
```

Notes:

1. If a < b is true, a is displayed, otherwise b.

2. The form of a statement using the ternary operator is:

```
(<relational expression> ? <value if true> : <value if false> )
```

3.5 Harder worked example.

(a) Write a program that will accept a given year. The program will then determine whether this year is a leap year and print an appropriate message. You may consider using the following rules for determining leap years.

- The year is divisible by 4 but not by 100.
- The year is divisible by 4 and by 400

(b) Continue this program by allowing a user to enter a number that represents a month. Given this month and the fact that the year is a leap year or not a leap year, will work out how many days in the month.

solution

<u>Example 32</u>

```cpp
/*    First version - Using only if statements                    */

#include <iostream>
using namespace std;

int main()
{
    int y, m, days;
    char leapyear;

    // Determine whether given year is a leap year
    cout << "Enter year ";
    cin >> y;
    if ((y % 4 == 0 and y % 100 != 100) or
        (y % 4 == 0 and y % 400 == 0))
    {
        leapyear = 't';
        cout << "Year " << y << " is a leapyear \n";
    }

    // Determine number of days in a given month
    cout << "\nEnter month (1-12) ";
    cin >> m;
    if (m == 4 or m == 6 or m == 9 or m == 11)
        days = 30;
    else if (m == 1 or m == 3 or m == 5 or m == 7 or
            m == 8 or m == 12)
        days = 31;
    else
        if (leapyear == 't')
            days = 29;
        else
            days = 28;

    cout << "\nNumber of days in month is " << days << endl;

    return 0;
}
```

```
Quincy 2005                                              _ |□| ×|
Enter year 1956
Year 1956 is a leapyear

Enter month (1-12) 5

Number of days in month is 31

Press Enter to return to Quincy...
```

48

3.6 The switch statement

In the previous worked example you will notice that the **if** statements became rather complicated. We even had problems fitting the conditions on one line. What is more, the test to see how many days to assign to February is a little confusing. Fortunately, there is a much neater solution to this problem and others like it. Part (b) of the previous program could be written as follows.

Example 33

```
/*    Second version - using switch statement to determine the days
in a month                                                       */

#include <iostream>
using namespace std;

int main()
{
      int y, m, days;
      char leapyear;

      // Determine whether given year is a leap year
      cout << "Enter year ";
      cin >> y;
      if ( (y % 4 == 0 and y % 100 != 100) or
           (y % 4 == 0 and y % 400 == 0))
      {
            leapyear = 't';
            cout << "Year " << y << " is a leapyear \n";
      }

      // Determine number of days in a given month
      cout << "\nEnter month (1-12) ";
      cin >> m;
      switch (m)
      {
            case 4:
            case 6:
            case 9:
            case 11:  days = 30; break;
            case 1:
            case 3:
            case 5:
            case 7:
            case 8:
            case 10:
            case 12:  days = 31; break;
            case 2:   if (leapyear == 't')
                      {
                            days = 29; break;
                      }
                      else
```

49

```
                    days = 28; break;
        default:  cout << "Invalid month " << endl; break;

    }

    cout << "\nNumber of days in month is " << days << endl;
    return 0;
}
```

Notes:

1. The variable being tested for in the switch statement and the data item following the keyword case must be an integer type. Note the data type char is also an integer type.

2. The keywords **and** and **or** are used instead of **&&** and **||** respectively.

3. A break statement is needed for each test, so that if a match is found the program will exit the switch statement.

4. The case **default:** is used if none of the cases are matched.

Exercise 3-2

1. (a) Write a program that will prompt a user to enter a number between 1 and 100

   (b) Test the number input to see if it is :-

   (i)   even
   (ii) odd
   (iii) greater than 50

   (c) Print appropriate responses for each of these tests.

2. Write a short program which will prompt a user for an exam mark in the range 1 - 100 and will respond by printing the mark and grade.

   The rules for awarding grades are as follows:

mark	grade
79 - 100	A
67 - 78	B
54 - 66	C
40 - 53	D
< 40	F

   Try writing two versions. One which uses an **if** statement, and another which uses a **case** statement.

3. Write a program that will input a person's height in centimetres (cm), and weight in kilograms (kg). The output from the program will be one of the following messages: underweight, normal, or overweight, using the criteria:

   Underweight: weight < height / 2.5
   Normal: height / 2.5 ≤ weight ≤ height / 2.3
   Overweight: height/ 2.3 < weight

4. (a) Modify the previous program used to calculate the roots of quadratic equations, so that all solutions are displayed to 2 decimal places.

   (b) Add an if statement to test for real solutions.
       (Note – for real solutions $b^2 > 4ac$)

5. Write a program that will input 3 names from the keyboard. The program will then display the 3 names in alphabetical order.

6. Write a program that allows a user to enter a date in the format dd/mm/yy and outputs the date in the format **month dd, year**.

   That is my birthday will be entered as: 22/05/56
   And will be output as: May 25, 1956

7. Write a program that takes as input a character (a, s, m, or d), followed by two integers. The program will calculate the sum, difference, product or quotient depending on the first character input.

Chapter 4 (Week 4)

An example coursework (A previous assignment)

4.1 Module 1 Assignment (Specification)

A local company wants to make a start at automating their payroll system. Currently the wage packets are made up individually. They get paid in cash and have a pay receipt that details hours worked, rate of pay, overtime and gross pay etc.

(a) Assuming a basic week is 37 hours, and that any time over this is to be treated as overtime which is to be paid as 1.5 times the standard rate. Write a program that will accept input from the user for :-

Employee name, hours worked, rate of pay

(b) The program will calculate:

- the overtime worked
- the basic salary (not including overtime)
- the overtime pay
- the gross pay (basic salary + overtime pay)

(c) The program will display each of the values input from the keyboard, together with the items calculated above.

(d) Add comments to document the program, and ensure that the program is readable by including appropriate indentation and spacing.

(e) Save your program. Call it **Payroll1**.

(f) Compile and Run your program. Make necessary corrections to make sure the program runs properly. Save the program again.

(g) Extend the program payroll1 by calculating the nett pay. Nett pay is calculated by deducting 25% tax from the taxable income. Assume that the first £60 of the weekly salary is non-taxable income. Don't forget to display the nett pay.

(h) Save this version of the program as **payroll2**.

Documentation required

1.   Name and describe the primitive data types in C++. Describe the basic properties of these data types and give an example of when each of them would be used.

2.   Produce a table to describe each variable you intend to declare in your program. The table should have the following format :-

Variable	Data type	Description

3.   Produce a program listing for payroll1 and payroll2.

4.   Produce a screen dump to demonstrate each program running.

5.   Explain the importance of testing programs. For each program, perform a simple dry run. Use a calculator to fill in the results of your dry run.

6.   Evaluate your program, and suggest improvements you could make if more time were available.

4.2 Sample solution (Old assignment)

4.2.1   Primitive data types in C++

I will not be answering this, as you will be asked to do this in your assignment. You should be able to find the answers in your notes. Alternatively, you should be encouraged to use books including this one.

4.2.2   Variables used

Variable name	Type	Description
empname	string	name of employee
hours	int	number of hours worked (nearest hour)
basicpay	float	amount of pay before overtime
overtime	int	number of hours overtime worked
overtimepay	float	amount of extra money earned for overtime
grosspay	float	total pay before tax deductions
taxablepay	float	amount of pay for which tax is paid
tax	float	amount of tax paid
nettpay	float	amount of pay after tax has been paid

4.3 Program listing

<u>Example 34</u>

```cpp
/*    Example solution to an old assignment 1
      that is being used to demonstrate what
      is expected of Access students

          Tony Hawken                              */

#include <iostream>
#include <string>
#include <iomanip>
using namespace std;

int main()
{
    string empname;
    int hours, overtime;
    float rate, basicpay, overtimepay, grosspay;

    // Input Employee name, hours worked and hourly rate (a)
    cout << "Employee name \t";
    getline(cin, empname);
    cout << "Hours worked \t";
    cin >> hours;
    cout << "hourly rate \t";
    cin >> rate;

    // Perform calculations  (b)
    if (hours >= 37)
    {
        basicpay = 37 * rate;
        overtime = hours - 37;
    }
    else
    {
        basicpay = hours * rate; // Assumes you only get paid
                                 // for hours worked
        overtime = 0;
    }
    overtimepay = overtime * rate * 1.5;
    grosspay = basicpay + overtimepay;

    // Display all data items.

    // Display input data
    cout << endl;  // start with a blank line
    cout << "Employee name \t\t" << empname << endl;
    cout << fixed << setw(7) <<setprecision(2);
    cout << "hours worked \t\t" << hours << endl;
```

```cpp
        cout << "hourly rate of pay \t" << rate << endl;

        // Display calculated results
        cout << "basic pay = \t\t" << basicpay << endl;
        cout << "overtime = \t\t" << overtime << endl;
        cout << "overtimepay = \t\t" << overtimepay << endl;
        cout << "grosspay = \t\t" << grosspay << endl << endl;

        // Calculate and display tax and nett pay  (g)
        float taxablepay, tax, nettpay;
        taxablepay = grosspay - 60.0;
        tax = 0.25 * taxablepay;
        nettpay = grosspay - tax;
        cout << "\nTaxable pay = \t\t" << taxablepay;
        cout << "\nIncome tax = \t\t" << tax;
        cout << "\nNett pay = \t\t" << nettpay << "\n\n";

        return 0;
}
```

The best way to obtain a program listing, is to open it in word. You can then paste it where you want in your documentation.

4.4 Screen dump

*A screen dump can be obtained by pressing the **Print Screen** key. This can be found at the top right hand side of the keyboard.*

*You should now use Paint. Then click on the **Paste** option.*

You would be advised to crop this screen dump to show only that part which is relevant. Once you have done this, cut out the highlighted part of the image you want to use.

*Now click on the **New** option, and then **Paste** the cropped image into the current window.*

*Finally save the picture to your folder using the **Save As** option.*
You will be shown how to do this in class. Please make sure that you are able to do this before you start your assignment.

An example screen dump from the above program has been inserted into this document.

```
Quincy 2005                                                      _ □ ×
Employee name     Fred Bloggs
Hours worked      47
hourly rate       8.75

Employee name               Fred Bloggs
hours worked                47
hourly rate of pay          8.75
basic pay =                 323.75
overtime =                  10
overtimepay =               131.25
grosspay =                  455.00


Taxable pay =               395.00
Income tax =                98.75
Nett pay =                  356.25

Press Enter to return to Quincy...._
```

4.5 Program Testing

4.5.1 Importance of testing programs

I will not be doing this, as you will be expected to do this yourself for your assignment. You will be encouraged to go to the library and take out relevant books.

You should be considering using the following:

- *A-level computing / IT text books*
- *GNVQ advanced or BTEC National computing / IT text books*
- *C++ programming text book. E.g. Programming with C++ by John Hubbard.*

You will be expected to write one or two paragraphs in your own words.

It would also be good practise to record the books used in the form of a bibliography.

4.5.2 Dry runs

To perform a dry-run you choose appropriate values for each of the variables in your program. This is referred to as test data. You then work out what you would expect the results of your program. You then compare these predicted results with those generated by running your program. This is normally done by creating a table with both sets of results and your comments.

Variable	Input value	Computed value (Calculator)	Output value (Computer)	Agreement
hours	47		47	Yes
rate	8.75		8.75	Yes
overtime		10	10	Yes
basicpay		323.75	323.75	Yes
overtimepay		131.25	131.25	Yes
grosspay		455	455	Yes
taxablepay		395	395	Yes
tax		98.75	98.75	Yes
nettpay		356.25	356.25	Yes

4.6   Evaluation

You need to write a paragraph or two to satisfy this criterion. The following evaluation is a good indication of what is expected at this level.

There are 7 values to be input from the keyboard.

The name is of type string. This is an obvious choice because this type of string is much easier to manipulate, should I wish to do so. The variables **hours** and **overtime** are declared as integers because it is assumed that you will need to work a whole number of hours. The other input values are declared as type float as these represent amounts of money. It is not necessary to use double as only two decimal places will be required.

It could be assumed that everyone will have to work a minimum of 37 hours. The basic pay would then determined by:

basicpay = 37 * rate

and overtime by:

overtime = hours – 37

This would favour the employees that do not work at least 37 hours, as they will be paid for this even if they work less.

In my version, the number of hours worked is tested, if greater than 37, the above calculations will be used, and if not their basic pay will be calculated by:

basicpay = hours * rate

The precision of all calculated floating point numbers need to be set to 2 decimal places, as these represent amounts of money. For that reason the following statement is used:

```
cout << fixed << setw(7) << setprecision(2);
```

The output is laid out in a very simple tabular format. If required it would be quite easy to rearrange this so that there were more columns in the table.

The program has been tested with a number of sets of test data, and in each case the program produces the correct results.

Chapter 5 (Week 5)

This week will be set aside to complete the assignment. It may also be used to consolidate material. You could start by reading the end of unit summary.

5.1 Tasks to finish

This week is to be used to finish your coursework. At this stage you should have all the skills that you need to complete your coursework. I will include a basic list of tasks that will summarise what you need to do.

1. Collect the necessary information. If there is insufficient information in this book, you will have to borrow a book from the library. The bibliography at the end of this book has some useful suggestions. You could also consider searching for topics on the Internet.

2. Create a bibliography listing your sources of information. This should be one of the first tasks you do, as it helps you structure your report. Also, if you have to reference your sources of information, you already have it written down. Don't forget to include page numbers of books used. That way it will be easy to find the information again.

3. At this stage the programs are likely to be quite simple and short. For that reason, you can probably get away with writing the program first without much of a design. I suggest that you build up the program incrementally, only adding a few new features at a time. At each stage save your work, then compile, link and run it. If successful, you can then add bits and continue as before.

4. You now need to start thinking about documentation. Start by reading through your program to make sure that you can understand it. Make sure that the indentation is consistent and that there are sufficient comments so that someone else will be able to read your program and understand what is going on.

5. In the example coursework given previously, you may have to write up about some item of theory. In the example given, you are asked to discuss the data types available in C++ and the importance of testing programs. All the information you need for a brief description is available in this book. If you want more detail you will have to look elsewhere.

6. Once the program is working you need to test it. In this case it is suggested that you perform a dry run.

7. If the tests suggest that the program is satisfactory, obtain a program listing and a screen dump. The program listing can be inserted into a Microsoft Word document, and so can the screen dump.

5.2 End of Unit Summary

1. All C++ programs contain a function called `main()`. This function returns an int. A return value of 0 indicates successful execution of the program

2. A program block is a collection of statements grouped together using { and }. Any variables declared within these brackets, are local to the block. This is often referred to as the scope of the variable

3. Programs usually have one or more #include directives. These are used to include the capability of using functions from a given library. If you write programs that use <iostream.h> rather than <iostream>, this indicates that you using an old, out-of-date compiler.

4. All programs using the current ANSI/ISO standard use namespaces. A namespace is a named collection of commands.

5. A program statement is a complete command. All program statements end with a semicolon.

6. C++ programs usually use stream input and output. The header file <iostream> is required to access the **cin** and **cout** streams, as well as the input operator **>>** and the output operator <<.

7. The member function **getline()** has to be used for strings with whitespace. This is because **cin** skips whitespace and terminates input when spaces are encountered.

8. Manipulators can be used to format both input and output. These require the header <iomanip>.

9. The current ANSI/ISO standard includes the string class for creating strings. These are preferable to **C-strings** which are declared using an array of char, or a pointer to char. These will be discussed in later units. The string class contains many operators and functions to manipulate strings. To use the functions to manipulate strings, the header <string> is required. To manipulate C-strings the header <cstring> is required.

10. The assignment statement is used to store a result in a given variable.

11. Variables cannot take the name of a reserve word. Nor can they start with a numeric digit, or a punctuation character. Also they cannot contain any punctuation character besides an underscore.

12. You should be familiar with arithmetic operators for integer, float and double operands. Operations such as division behave differently according to whether the operands are of integer or not.

13. The scope of a variable is the extent of those parts of the program that can access that variable.

14. Variables that can be accessed from anywhere in the program are said to have global scope and are called **global** variables.

15. If a variable is declared within a program block, we say that the scope of the variable is within that block. We call such a variable a **local** variable.

16. Comments. There are two types. C++ comments include the symbol //. Everything after // is ignored by the compiler for the rest of the current line. C-style comments start with /* and end with */. Everything in between these two characters are ignored by the compiler.

17. Program indentation is for readability. Programs must be consistently indented to make them more readable.

18. C++ is case sensitive. All keywords are always written in lower-case.

19. Use of **if** and **switch** statements to indicate selection. In C++ the switch statement is not very powerful. It can only be used to test variables that are of integer type. Remember that char is also an integer type.

Part 2

Further C++ programming

Aims

After completing this 5-week unit, you will be able to do the following:

Control structures

Identify and use appropriate iteration methods to solve particular programming problems.

Know how to, and be able to terminate a loop in a number of different ways.

Functions

Write programs that use functions and include all of the following: function prototype, function definition, and function call.

Pass data to functions using two different parameter-passing methods.

User interface

Produce clear and appropriate prompts for entering data, neatly formatted output and output in the form of a table.

Use functions to provide input and output.

Design and Documentation

Analyse a problem and be able to write up the analysis.

Produce a design using both pseudo-code and structure charts.

Produce documentation that describes the functions in your programs

Chapter 6 (week 6)

6.1   Iteration

There are many programming problems that require the same sequence of statements to be executed again and again, either a fixed number of times or an indefinite number of times. One way to do this would be to type in the same code many times. However, this is very impractical, especially if the code needs to be repeated many times. Also, we don't always know in advance how many times the statements are to be repeated.

The repeated execution of the same statements is often called looping (or iteration). If the number of repetitions is known in advance, the **for** statement is probably the most appropriate to use.

In all other situations, either **do** or **while** statements should be used.

6.2 Looping a fixed number of times (for loops)

The **for** statement is used where it is necessary to repeat a section of code a fixed number of times.

Example 35

```
#include <iostream>
using namespace std;

int main()
{
     string name;
     cout << "Enter name : ";
     cin >> name;
     for (int c = 0; c < 100; c++)
          cout << name;

     return 0;
}
```

Here **cout << name;** is repeated 100 times which results in the value of name being printed 100 times.

A previous program that we looked at involved the calculation of 5 numbers input at the keyboard. It contained code like this:

```
cout << "Enter 5 numbers ";
cin >> a >> b >> c >> d >> e;
average = (a + b + c + d + e) / 5.0;
cout << "Average value is " << average;
```

This program does the job intended. But, it is a bad example of programming, as it is difficult to modify to satisfy similar problems. What do we do if we want a program to calculate the average of 100, 1000 or more numbers?

You will notice in this form there is a pattern that is repeated 5 times. Each time we input a number. In C++ we can repeat statements a fixed number of times using a **for** statement. We could for instance write:

```
for (int c = ; c < 100; c++)
{
        cout << "Enter next number : ";
        cin >> num;
}
```

The variable called **c**, is called a control variable and is used to count how many times the statement(s) are to be repeated. In this example, 100 times. The control variable **c** starts with a value of (initial value), and each time the program loops, a number is input and **c** is incremented by 1 until 100 is reached (final value).

We now have a problem in that every time we execute

```
cin >> num;
```

we lose the number previously entered. We need to adopt a slightly different strategy.

```
int num, total = 0;
for (int c = 0; c < 100; c++)
{
        cout << "Enter number : ";
        cin >> num;
            total += num;
}
```

Here we have included a variable called **total**, so that we can get a running total each time we enter a number. For each repetition of the **for** loop the number input to **num** is added to the previous total. Done this way, it doesn't matter if **num** is overwritten. Notice how total is set to 0 initially. Why is this? ...

The final program can now be written as:

Example 36

```cpp
#include <iostream>
using namespace std;

int main()
{
    int c, num, total = 0;

    for (c = 0; c < 5; c++)
    {
        cout << "Enter number : ";
        cin >> num;
        total += num
    }

    float average = static_cast<float> (total) / c ;
    cout << "Average value is " << average;

    return 0;
}
```

```
CN  Quincy 2005                                              _ □ ✕
Enter number : 8
Enter number : 6
Enter number : 4
Enter number : 3
Enter number : 5
total = 26
c = 6
average = 5.2

Press Enter to return to Quincy...
```

This version is a much better version and should we want a program to calculate the average of 100 or 1000 numbers it is an easy matter to change the program.

Note the presence of `static_cast<float>(total)` in the last assignment statement. This converts the result of total to a float before calculating the average. Without this **cast**, the result stored in average would be an **integer**.

This program assumes that we know in advance how many numbers you are going to enter. If a different number of numbers is required each time you run your program, you could at least enter at the keyboard how many numbers you intend to process. The program above can be easily modified to produce the following.

Example 37

```
#include <iostream>
using namespace std;

int main()
{
    int n;
    cout << "How many numbers do you have ";
    cin >> n;
    int c, num, total = 0;
    for (c = 0; c < n; c++)
    {
        cout << "Enter number ";
        cin >> num;
        total += num;
    }
    float average = static_cast<float> (total) / c ;
    cout << "Average value is " << average;

    return 0;
}
```

Note:

In programs that predate the current ANSI/ISO standard, it was normal to write

```
    float average = (float) total / c;
```

In place of:

```
        float average = static_cast<float> (total) / c ;
```

The MinGW C++ compiler will however accept either version.

67

Choosing a different problem, we can also make other uses of the control variable.

Example 38

```
#include <iostream>
using namespace std;

int main()
{
    cout << " Multiplication Tables";
    cout << "  --------------------";
    cout << "Enter number (table you want to practice) ";
    cin >> num;
    for (int c = 1; c <= 10; c++)
        cout << c << " * " << num << " = " << (c * num) << "\n";

    return 0;
}
```

In this example the control variable **c** is also used in the calculation **c * num**.

In general, the for statement can be written as:

for (<initialisation > ; <test form terminatuion> ; <post action>)
         <statement to be repeated>

The code below illustrates how you can count backwards.

```
for (int n = 10;  n >= 1; n--)
        cout << n << "   ";
```

Exercise 6-1

1. Write a program that allows a user to enter their name. The program will then print out their name 5 times.

2. Write a program to convert a temperature measured in degrees Centigrade to degrees Fahrenheit. Modify this program so that the temperature in Centigrade is worked out for all temperatures 0 - 100C.

3. Write a program to compute factorials given that :-

    5 factorial (5!) = 5 × 4 × 3 × 2 × 1

4. Write a program that will test for prime numbers.

    (a)   A prime number has two divisors only (1 and itself). Start by testing all the numbers that divide into the given number.

    (b)   You may want to use the % operator to test for a remainder on division, and the operator / for integer division.

    (c)   A nice extension would be to print a listing of all the factors in ascending order.

5. Roman numerals are notoriously difficult to perform any form of calculation with. They are principally used to record numbers.

    A roman number is constructed with the following numerals:

Roman numeral:	I	V	X	L	C	D	M
Arabic equivalent:	1	5	10	50	100	500	1000

    A roman number is constructed by adding these numerals. To make things even more difficult there is an additional rule; If a smaller numeral is placed in front of a larger numeral, you subtract the value of the smaller numeral from the value of the larger numeral.

    e.g The year of my birthday (1956) is represented as MCMLVI.

    Write a program that allows you to enter an integer representing a year, and will convert this year to its equivalent Roman number. Test your program with the year 1956.

6.3 Sequences and Series

A set of numbers written in a definite order and with a constant relationship between terms is called a sequence.

The following are examples of sequences:

(i)   2, 6, 10, 14, 18, 22

(ii)   1, 4, 9, 16, 25, 36

One way of generalising such sequences, is to define a general term. That is, an arithmetic expression that can be used to calculate any desired term.

Referring to sequence (i) it is not always easy to make such a generalisation. You will however notice that there is a constant difference of +4 between terms.

In other words we have $x_1 = 2$ (initial term), $x_2 = x_1 + 4 = 2 + 4 = 6$, $x_3 = x_2 + 4 = 10$ and generally $x_{n+1} = x_n + 4$. A general formula like this is called a recurrence relation or iterative formula.

The only two pieces of information we require are:

(i)   Initial value is 2

(ii)   General rule is add 4 to get the next term

We can use this information to calculate as many terms in the sequence as we please. If we were to use a **for** loop, then **n** would be used as a control variable. To calculate and print out the first 10 terms we could write the following:

Example 39

```cpp
#include <iostream>
using namespace std;

int main()
{
    cout << "n\t\tterm";
    term = 2;        // Set initial term equal to 2 }
    for (int n = 2; n <= 10; n++)
    {
        term += 4;         // Add 4 to get next term
        cout << n << "\t\t" << term;
    }

    return 0;
}
```

Referring to sequence (ii) it is much easier to state a general term, than to find the relationship between successive terms. We have here a sequence of square numbers. The general term then is $x_n = n^2$.

If the terms of a sequence are added to form a sum, the result is called a series.

The following are also examples of series:

(i)   2 + 6 + 10 + 14 + 18 + 22 + ...
(ii)   1 + 4 + 9 + 16 + 25 + 36 + ...

The sum of the first 10 terms of series (i) can be calculated as follows:

Example 40

```
#include <iostream>
using namespace std;

int main()
{
      int term = 2;
      int sum = 2; // Initial term is 2, so sum of one term is 2
      for (int n = 2; n <= 10; n++)
      {
            term += 4;
            Sum += term;
      }
      cout << "Sum of 10 terms is " << sum;

      return 0;
}
```

The sum of the first 10 terms of the second series can be calculated as follows:

Example 41

```
#include <iostream>
using namespace std;

int main()
{
      int sum = 0;
      for (int n = 1; n <= 10; n++)
            sum += n * n;

      cout << "Sum of 10 terms is " << sum;

      return 0;
}
```

This also is a very easy modification of the program that generates the sequence.

6.4 While loops

All of these programs can be rewritten using **while** loops, which can be considered to be a more general form of **for** loop.

Now consider the following sequence.

$$1/1 , 1/2 , 1/3 , 1/4 , 1/5 , 1/6 , ... , 1/n$$

Using a **for** loop it can be written as:

```
cout << "n\t\tterm" << endl;
for (int n = 1; n <= 10; n++)
    cout << n << "\t\t" << (1 / n) << endl;
```

Such a sequence is said to be **convergent**, as each successive term approaches a certain value. In this case zero. Sequences that don't converge are said to be **divergent**.

The same result can be obtained using a **while** loop as follows:

Example 42

```
#include <iostream>
using namespace std;

int main()
{
    cout << "n\t\tterm" << endl;
    int n = 1;
    while (n <= 10)
    {
        cout << n << "\t\t" << (1.0 / n) << endl;
        n++;
    }
    return 0;
}
```

```
Quincy 2005                                          _ □ ×
n               term
1               1
2               0.5
3               0.333333
4               0.25
5               0.2
6               0.166667
7               0.142857
8               0.125
9               0.111111
10              0.1

Press Enter to return to Quincy..._
```

Here you will notice that the control variable **n** has to be initialised and incremented to count the number of terms. This is obviously more difficult than using a **for** loop.

However, when you use a **while** loop, the condition does not have to involve the control variable. For instance, we could terminate the **while** loop when the term goes below a certain size.

Example 43

```cpp
#include <iostream>
using namespace std;

int main()
{
    cout << "n\t\tterm\n";
    int n = 1;
    while (1.0 / n > 0.09999)
    {
        cout << n << "\t\t" << (1.0 / n) << endl;
        n++;
    }

    return 0;
}
```

```
Quincy 2005                                                  _ □ ×
n               term
1               1
2               0.5
3               0.333333
4               0.25
5               0.2
6               0.166667
7               0.142857
8               0.125
9               0.111111
10              0.1

Press Enter to return to Quincy...
```

In this example, the output generated is exactly the same as for the previous two programs

The general format of the **while** statement is as follows:

> **while (<condition>)**
> **<Statement>**

Here <statement> is executed while <condition> is true. In other words, the loop terminates when <condition> becomes false.

6.5 Using a break to terminate a loop

The equation $x^3 + x = 11$ has a solution slightly greater than 2. Find the solution to 2 decimal places by calculating $y = x^3 + x$ for values of x increasing in steps of 0.01 from x = 2, stopping when y first exceeds 11.

Example 44

```cpp
#include <iostream>
using namespace std;

int main()
{
    cout << "x" << "\t" << "y" << endl;
    double x = 2.0, y;
    for(; ; )
    {
        y = x * x * x + x;
        cout << x << "\t" << y << endl;
        if (y >= 11)
            break;
        else
            x += 0.01;
    }
    return 0;
}
```

Notes:

1. The statement header `for(; ; )` denotes an infinite loop

2. The break statement is needed to terminate the loop.

```
C:\ Quincy 2005                                    _ □ ×
x       y
2       10
2.01    10.1306
2.02    10.2624
2.03    10.3954
2.04    10.5297
2.05    10.6651
2.06    10.8018
2.07    10.9397
2.08    11.0789

Press Enter to return to Quincy...
```

Exercise 6-2

1. Write a program to work out a person's change. It is assumed that they only have a £10 note to pay this. The required change should then be calculated so that a minimum number of coins are given. No notes are given as change.

Analysis of problem

1. Easier if change required is converted to pence.
2. Coins currently available are £2, £1, 50p, 20p, 10p, 5p, 2p, 1p.
3. Need to keep a coin count for each type of coin.

Suggested program structures

1. Assignment to store coin counts and amount of change.
2. **while** loops to calculate number of coins required.
3. **if** statements to determine coins to be printed.

2. A calculator or for that matter any computer uses a limited amount of storage to store numbers. You may have discovered the problem of overflow while using a calculator. You try to perform a calculation and the result is too large to fit in the allocated space. Instead of obtaining the correct result you usually just get an error message.

If we think of how a real number is represented this should give us an idea to tackle this problem. A real number is made up of two parts a mantissa and exponent.

A real number is then represented as:

$$num = mantissa \times 2^{exponent}$$

This is similar to representing a number in standard form. In standard form we work in base 10. If we were to multiply this number by 10, this can be achieved by adding one to the exponent

Using this idea of standard form write a program which can compute very large factorials. Use your program to compute 720 factorial.

6.6 The do loop

Suppose we want to work out the average of all numbers until there are no more numbers to enter. We now have the problem of telling the program there is no more data to enter. This can be achieved using a **data terminator**. That is we can choose a value which can't possibly be a valid data value for the problem in question and then test the value entered each time.

The following is a first attempt at calculating the total.

Example 45

```cpp
#include <iostream>
using namespace std;

int main()
{
    int num, total = 0, c = 0;
    do
    {
        cout << "Enter number : ";
        cin >> num;
        total += num;
        c++;
    }
    while (num != -1);

    cout << "Total sum is " << total << endl;
    float average = static_cast<float> (total) / c;
    cout << "Average is " << average;

    return 0;
}
```

```
Quincy 2005                                          _ □ ✕
Enter number : 5
Enter number : 6
Enter number : 7
Enter number : 4
Enter number : -1
Total sum is 21
Average is 4.2
Press Enter to return to Quincy...
```

The above can be interpreted as meaning repeat the statements between **do** and the **while** clause, until **num** is set to -1. This is similar to the while statement except that the test is done after executing the statements.

There are two things wrong with it. The value of **total** is wrong. In this example, the data terminator 1 has been added to the total. Likewise, the value of the number count (c) is 1 too many for the same reason.

You could get round the problem as follows:

Example 46

```cpp
#include <iostream>
using namespace std;

int main()
{
    int total = 0, c = 0;
    int num;

    do
    {
        cout << "Enter number :   ";
        cin >> num;
        if (num != -1)
        {
            total += num;
            c += 1;
        }

    } while (num != -1);

    cout << "Total = " << total << endl;

    float average = static_cast<float> (total) / c;
    cout << "Average is " << (average);

    return 0;
}
```

```
C:\ Quincy 2005                                        _ □ ✕
Enter number :  5
Enter number :  6
Enter number :  7
Enter number :  4
Enter number :  -1
Total = 22
Average is 5.5
Press Enter to return to Quincy...
```

In this example, the terminating number is not added to the total, nor the count incremented, because the current number input is tested first.

A more elegant solution would involve rearranging the statements.

Example 47

```cpp
#include <iostream>
using namespace std;

int main()
{
    int num, total = 0, c = 0;
    cout << "Enter number : ";
    cin >> num;

    do
    {
        total += num;
        c++;
        cout << "Enter number : ";
        cin >> num;
    }while (num != -1);

    cout << "Total = " << total << endl;
    float average = static_cast<float> (total) / c;
    cout << "Average is " << average;

    return 0;
}
```

This gives the same output as example 46.

6.7 Terminating input by testing cin

In C++ it is not necessary to use a data terminator as discussed previously. Instead, input can be terminated using a non-numeric character. To do this you should test whether the previous input using **cin** was successful. The following program fragment performs the input within the header of a while loop.

Example 48

```
#include <iostream>
using namespace std;

int main()
{
    int num, total = 0;
    cout << "Enter a list of numbers terminated by" << endl;
    cout << "an alphabetic character" << endl;

    while (cin >> num)
        total += num;
    cout << "total is " << total << endl;

    return 0;
}
```

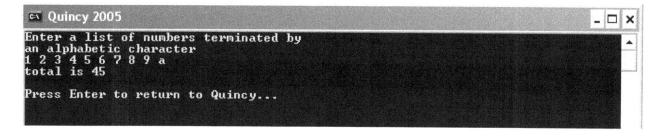

Notes:

1. The stream operator **cin** has a return value that can be tested – true or false. It can be tested with an **if** or **while** statement.

6.8 Nested Loops

One of the earliest examples of repetition we looked at involved the production of multiplication tables. See Example 38.

This would output a sequence of numbers, which would be multiples of the number chosen, with two spaces between each number.

You may now want to modify this program to repeat this for all the numbers 1 - 10 rather than just one number. This could be achieved by having an additional control variable and repeating the code 10 times.

Example 49

```cpp
#include <iostream>
#include <iomanip>
using namespace std;

int main()
{
    for (int row = 1; row <= 10; row++)
    {
        for (int col = 1; col <= 10; col++)
            cout << setw(6) << (row * col);
        cout << endl;
    }
    return 0;
}
```

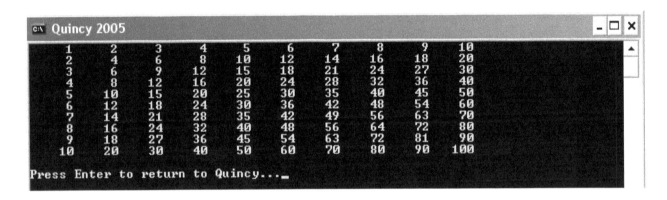

Exercise 6-3

1. Write a program that can be used to determine the minimum, maximum and mean value of a set of positive numbers. The numbers are to be entered from the keyboard, and termination will occur when a negative number is read.

2. Adapt the above program. In this case, test cin to determine when to terminate the loop.

Chapter 7 (Week 7)

7.1 Use of functions in C++

As programs get larger, it is important to be able to split the program into smaller components. Most programming languages achieve this by providing constructs such as functions or procedures that break the program up into a number of self-contained modules that communicate with each other. Each of these modules should be able to perform a useful task and should be available for use anywhere in the program. Such a facility makes a program easier to develop, easier to debug and improves the readability of the program.

In very simple terms:

1. A **function** is a block of code containing statements that perform a calculation and returns an answer called the **return value**.

2. A **procedure** is a block of code containing statements, that when executed perform some actions that satisfy a certain task.

3. The C++ language only has functions. The equivalent of a procedure in C++, is a function that returns **void**.

4. Functions that return a void are typically used to calculate a result and/or produce output. They can also be used to input data. In languages such as Pascal these are called procedures.

7.2 An introduction to functions

You have probably met functions already in the mathematics classroom.

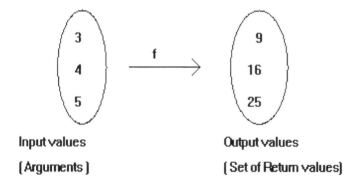

Input values

(Arguments)

Output values

(Set of Return values)

The above function f computes the square number of its input value.

Using standard mathematical notation, we could state:

```
f(3) = 9, f(4) = 16, f(5) = 25
```

There are built-in functions available within the C++ language and standard libraries available to C++. There exists the standard C library called <cmath>.

This contains those functions useful for mathematics. This is available also to all C++ programs, As C++ programs are able to use all the standard C libraries.

The following program illustrates the use of sqrt().

Example 50

```cpp
#include <iostream>
#include <cmath>
using namespace std;

int main()
{
    int c = 130;
    double sq;
    cout << "The square root of " << c;
    cout << " is " << sqrt(c) << endl;
    sq = sqrt(c);
    cout << "Value of sq is " << sq << endl;
    return 0;
}
```

```
Quincy 2005                                    _ □ ×
The square root of 130 is 11.4018
Value of sq is 11.4018

Press Enter to return to Quincy...
```

Notes:

1. `#include <cmath>` is required to provide the **function prototype** for the sqrt() function.

2. The **function prototype** for sqrt() is `double sqrt(double);`

3. Within the main function there is a function call - sqrt(c)

4. This has an actual parameter called c which is declared as an integer.

5. The prototype for sqrt() states that the parameter should be a double. So any values entered will automatically be converted to a double.

6. The return value for sqrt() is declared to be a double. That is why the variable sq has to be declared as a double.

7. The parameter passing mechanism is called **call-by-value**.

7.3 Mathematical functions

The C++ library provides an excellent collection of mathematical functions, that compare very favourably with those in the Fortran language – which has for a long time had a good reputation for numerical computations. All functions in <cmath> use double precision arithmetic, so that the answers obtained are more accurate than most other languages.

The following functions are declared in <cmath>

Powers

```
sqrt(x), pow(x, p), exp(x)   (p has to be an int)
```

Trigonometric functions

```
sin(x), cos(x), tan(x)
```
            (x measured in radians)

Inverse trigonometric functions

```
asin(x), acos(x), atan(x)
```

Logarithms

```
log(x), log10(x)
```

Misc other

```
abs(x), ceil(x), floor(x)
```

All functions declared in <cmath> return a double.

7.4 User-defined functions

In the context of the examples, which follow, we will discuss:

- function declaration (function prototype) and function definition
- function header and function body
- return value
- function call
- parameters and parameter passing

Example 51

```cpp
#include <iostream>
#include <iostream>

float ctof(int);    // function prototype (declaration)

using namespace std;

int main()
{
    int c = 37;
    float f;
    // Store result of function call to a variable
    f = ctof(c);        //function call
    cout << c << " degrees C is " << f << endl;
    // Output return value of function call
    cout << c << " degrees C is " << ctof(c);

    return 0;
}


//given a temperature in Centigrade return temperature in
// Fahrenheit
float ctof(int c)        // function definition
{
    float f = 9 * c / 5 + 32;
    return f;
}
```

Notes:

1. The function prototype **float ctof(int);** is a declaration that states that there is a function called ctof, and that this has one parameter that is of type int, and that it returns a float.

2. The prototype of a function matches the function header of the function definition.

3. It is the function definition that specifies what action the function will take.

4. The function is executed with a function call. The function call **f = ctof(c);** passes the value of the variable c to the function. This parameter passing mechanism is called "**Call by Value**"

5. Inside the function, the value of c is treated like a local variable. This value of c used to calculate f. The value of f is then returned to the calling function.

The following example program includes a function that returns a string containing the day of the month for a given day number.

Example 52

```cpp
#include <iostream>
#include <string>
using namespace std;

string getday(int);        // function prototype (declaration)

int main()
{
    int n;
    cout << "Enter a number 1-7 : " ;
    cin >> n;
    // Output includes a function call
    cout << "day number " << n << " is " << getday(n) << endl;
    return 0;
}

// Given a number 1 to 7, return the day of the week
string getday(int n)       // function definition
{
    string day;
    switch (n)
    {
        case 1:    day = "Monday"; break;
        case 2:    day = "Tuesday"; break;
        case 3:    day = "Wednesday"; break;
        case 4:    day = "Thursday"; break;
        case 5:    day = "Friday"; break;
        case 6:    day = "Saturday"; break;
        case 7:    day = "Sunday"; break;
        default:   day = "Invalid day";
    }
    return day;
}
```

The following example defines two functions. The function `min()` has two parameters. The smallest of these values is returned. In the case of `max()`, this also has two parameter. It returns the larger of these two values.

Example 53

```cpp
#include <iostream>
using namespace std;

int min(int, int);
int max(int, int);

int main()
{
    int a, b;
    cout << "Enter two whole numbers : ";

    cin >> a >> b;
    cout << "smallest number is " << min(a, b) << endl;
    cout << "Enter two numbers : ";
    cin >> a >> b;
    cout << "Largest number is " << max(a, b) << endl;

    return 0;
}

//return the minimum of two numbers
int min(int x, int y)
{
    if (x < y)
        return x;
    else
        return y;
}

//return the maximum of two numbers
int max(int x, int y)
{
    if (x > y)
        return x;
    else
        return y;
}
```

Exercise 7-1

1. Write a function to compute the cube of a number. You should declare the function prototype :-

   ```
   double cube(double);
   ```

   Include one or more function calls to test your function `cube()`.

2. Write a function to compute the hypotenuse of a right-angled triangle given the other two sides. Test it out by printing the length of the 3 sides of the triangle.

3. Write a program, to perform a temperature conversion for values 1^0 C – 100^0C. The program should have a function to perform the conversion, and will print out both temperatures (Centigrade and Fahrenheit) in a neat table to 2 decimal places.

4. Write a function with the following function prototype

   ```
   int sumsquares( int n);
   ```

   The function will return an int which is the sum of the squares of the integers 1 to n. Write a program that uses this function to print out the sum of the first 20 squares, and the sum of the first 100 squares.

5. The combination function often referred to as $_nC_r$ in older mathematics textbooks, computes the number of **unordered r element sub-sets** from a set of **n elements**.

   In functional notation this function can be written as :-

   $$C(n, r) = \frac{n!}{r!\,(n - r)!} \qquad \text{Where n! = n factorial} = n \times (n-1) \times (n-2) \times (n-3) \times \ldots \ldots \times 3 \times 2 \times 1$$

   In newer textbooks $_nC_r$ is represented as $\begin{bmatrix} n \\ r \end{bmatrix}$

   (a) Write a program that includes a factorial function

   (b) Add to this a combination function that uses the above formula

   (c) Used these functions to compute the binomial coefficients for a given power

   An example of a binomial expansion follows:

   $$(x+y)^5 = \begin{bmatrix} 5 \\ 0 \end{bmatrix}(x+y)^0 + \begin{bmatrix} 5 \\ 1 \end{bmatrix}(x+y)^1 + \begin{bmatrix} 5 \\ 2 \end{bmatrix}(x+y)^2 + \begin{bmatrix} 5 \\ 3 \end{bmatrix}(x+y)^3 + \begin{bmatrix} 5 \\ 4 \end{bmatrix}(x+y)^4$$

   $$+ \begin{bmatrix} 5 \\ 5 \end{bmatrix}(x+y)^5$$

7.5 Functions that return void

In other programming languages, procedures are available as well as functions. A function that returns a void is equivalent to a procedure. These functions are typically used to produce either input or output. They can also be used to perform calculations and the print out the results rather than return a single value that can either be printed out or stored in a variable.

Example 54 - Enter employee details

```
#include <iostream>
using namespace std;

void enterdetails(void);
char name[20];              // global variables
float rate, hours;          // can be accessed from anywhere
                            // in the program

int main()
{
    enterdetails();       //function call
    // Display details
    cout << "Name : " << name << endl;
    cout << "Rate of pay = " << rate << " per hour" << endl;
    cout << "Number of hours worked = " << hours << endl;
    return 0;
}

void enterdetails(void)
{
    cout << "Enter employee name : ";
    cin.getline(name, 20);
    cout << "Enter hourly rate of pay : ";
    cin >> rate;
    cout << "Enter number of hours worked : ";
    cin >> hours;
}
```

Notes :

1. The scope of the variables name, rate and hours is **global** because they are declared before any of the functions are defined. They can be accessed anywhere in the program from within any function in the program.

2. In the function enterdetails(), the variables name, rate and hours are not declared. They are therefore assumed to be global.

7.6 Call –by-reference

Generally speaking, it is bad programming practice to use global variables in this manner, as they could be updated by other parts of the program without the programmer knowing about it. A better technique would be to use reference variables. The following program illustrates **call-by-reference** parameter passing. This method is much safer.

Example 55

```cpp
#include <iostream>
#include <string>
using namespace std;

void enterdetails(string, float&, float&);
void displaydetails(string, float&, float&);

int main()
{
    char * empname;
    float rateofpay, hoursworked;
    enterdetails(empname, rateofpay, hoursworked);
    displaydetails(empname, rateofpay, hoursworked);

    return 0;
}

void enterdetails(string name, float& rate, float& hours)
{
    cout << "Enter employee name : ";
    getline(cin, name);
    cout << "Enter hourly rate of pay : ";
    cin >> rate;
    cout << "Enter number of hours worked : ";
    cin >> hours;
}

void displaydetails(string name, float& rate, float& hours)
{
    cout << "\nEmployee name : \t\t" << name;
    cout << "\nHourly rate of pay : \t\t" << rate;
    cout << "\nNumber of hours worked : \t" << hours;
}
```

Notes:

1. When the function `enterdetails()` is called, it is supplied with the actual parameters `empname`, `rateofpay` and `hoursworked`.

2. The function definition for `enterdetails()` has **formal parameters** `name`, `rate` and `hours`. Theses are aliases for the **actual parameters** `empname`, `rate` and `hours`.

3. When you enter data to any of the parameters name, rate, and pay you are really updating the variables `empname`, `rateofpay` and `hoursworked`.

7.7 A longer example

Most books have an ISBN that have 10 digits and uses a modulo 11 check digit for validation purposes. The following are examples of valid ISBNs:

1-85805-080-4
0 521 29101 1

You will notice that the number is punctuated by either hyphens or spaces. It doesn't matter where the hyphens are. The digit furthest on the right is called the check digit. The rule for obtaining the check digit is as follows:

1. Each of the digits except the check digit is given a weight. Starting at the right, the weight is 2, to the left of this the digit has a weight of 3 and so on.

2. Each of the digits is multiplied by its weight, and all of these products are summed.

3. This sum is divided by 11, and the remainder kept.

4. The checksum is calculated by subtracting the remainder from 11.

If an ISBN is valid, it needs to have 10 digits (once spaces and hyphens have been removed) and the checksum needs to equal the check digit.

The following program validates an ISBN.

Example 56

```
#include <iostream>
#include <string>
using namespace std;

void removeHyphens(string &);
void removeSpaces(string &);
bool validate(string);

int main()
{
    string isbn;
    cout << "Enter and ISBN (Can contain spaces or hyphens) : ";
    getline(cin, isbn);
    cout << isbn << endl;
    bool valid = validate(isbn);
    if(valid)
        cout << "Valid ISBN " << endl;

    return 0;
```

```cpp
}

void removeHyphens(string & isbn)
{
     int n = isbn.length();
     for(int c = 0; c < n; c++)
     if (isbn[c] == '-')
          isbn.erase(c,1);
}

void removeSpaces(string & isbn)
{
     int n = isbn.length();
     for(int c = 0; c < n; c++)
     if (isbn[c] == ' ')
          isbn.erase(c,1);
}

bool validate(string isbn)
{
     removeHyphens(isbn);
     removeSpaces(isbn);
     if (isbn.length() == 10)
     {
          int sum = 0; int digit;

          for(int c = 0; c < 9; c++)
          {
               digit = isbn[c] - 48;
               sum += digit * (10 - c);
          }
          sum %= 11;
          int checksum = 11 - sum;

          int lastdigit;        //Check digit
          if ((isbn[9] == 'X')||(isbn[9] == 'x'))
               lastdigit = 10;
          else
               lastdigit = isbn[9] - 48;

          if (checksum == lastdigit)
               return true;
          else
               return false;
     }
}
```

```
C:\Program Files\quincy\bin\quincy.exe

Enter and ISBN (Can contain spaces or hyphens) : 1-85805-080-4
1-85805-080-4
Valid ISBN

Press Enter to return to Quincy...
```

Notes:

1. The function `length()` is required to obtain the length of the string.

2. You can access individual characters in a string using the subscript operator `[]`. So for instance `isbn[0]` will allow you to access the first character, `isbn[1]`, the second and so on.

3. The erase() function can be used to remove 1 or more characters.

4. The clause `if(isbn[c] == ' ')` tests whether the character in position c is a space.

5. The statement `isbn.erase(c,1);` will erase 1 character starting at position c. This statement can be used to remove either hyphens or spaces within the ISBN.

6. The statement `digit = isbn[c] - 48;` is used to convert a character to an integer . It works because the ASCII code for 0 is 48. So if you subtract 48 from any character that corresponds to a numeric digit, you get the number itself.

7. The checksum is initially worked out by summing the product of all the numeric digits, excluding the check digit. This is achieved with the statement:

   `sum += digit * (10 - c);`

8. The remainder is obtained using the modulus operator `%`. Finally this value is subtracted from 11 to obtain the checksum.

7.8 Recursion

Recursion is the technique of describing something in terms of itself. So a recursive procedure or function is said to be self-referential. Recursion is an alternative method to iterative algorithms.

The simplest example that appears in many books dealing with the topic of recursion is factorials. One way of describing a factorial is to give an example like the following and then generalise it.

$$5! = 5 \times 4 \times 3 \times 2 \times 1 \qquad \text{(where ! is a short-hand for factorial)}$$

More generally we could say :-

$$n! = n \times (n-1) \times (n-2) \times \ldots \ldots \times 3 \times 2 \times 1$$

To be more accurate we would also have to state that $0! = 1$.

We could implement this non-recursively using the following function:

```
int factorial(int n)
{
    int product = 1;
    for(int c = 1; c <= n; c++)
        product *= c;
    return product;
}
```

But, if you look at the first definition again, you will notice that it can easily be expanded as follows:

$$n! = n \times (n-1) \times (n-2) \times \ldots \ldots \ldots \times 3 \times 2 \times 1$$

$$n! = n \times (n-1)!$$
$$(n-1)! = (n-1) \times (n-2)!$$
$$(n-2)! = (n-2) \times (n-3)!$$
.
.
.
$$3! = 3 \times 2!$$
$$2! = 2 \times 1!$$
$$1! = 1 \times 0! \qquad \text{and we know what } 0! = 1 \text{ by definition.}$$

These expressions are called recurrence relations.

If we take the most general expression which is:

$$n! = n \times (n-1)!$$

and the terminating condition $0! = 1$, we can easily write a recursive function to do the same thing.

Such a recursive function may look like this:

```
int factorial(int n)
{
    if (n == 1)
        return 1;
    else
        return (n * factorial(n-1));
}
```

Now is the time to explain how recursion works.

Recursive evaluation of 5!

		Stack		Stack	Pop items off stack
	0!	1		1	
	1!	1 × 0!		1× 1	1
	2!	2 × 1!		2 × 1	2
	3!	3 × 2!		3 × 2	6
	4!	4 × 3!		4 × 6	24
Push items on stack	5!	5 × 4!		5 × 24	120

Each time a recursive call is made, it is stored on the stack ready to be used at a later time. When a termination condition arises (0! = 1) this stops. The first item is popped off the stack and the value substituted into the expression below. This continues until the last item on the stack is removed. By this time 5! has been evaluated.

The complete program looks like this

Example 57

```
#include <iostream>
using namespace std;

int factorial(int);

int main()
{
    cout << factorial(5);
    return 0;
}

int factorial(int n)
{
    if (n == 1)
        return 1;
    else
        return (n * factorial(n-1));
}
```

```
Quincy 2005                                              _ □ ×
120
Press Enter to return to Quincy..._
```

Exercise 7-2

1 (a) Write a function to display a menu such as:

> MENU
> -------
> 1.   Play Space Invaders
> 2.   Play PACMAN
> 3.   Play Super Mario
> 4.   Quit Menu

(b) Test the function by including in your program a function call

(c) Modify your main program so that a user is prompted to enter a number corresponding to the desired choice.

(d) Include this in a while loop which terminates when they choose the option to quit the menu.

2. Fibonacci numbers can be computed by adding together the two previous numbers. The following is a Fibonacci series:

> 1, 1, 2, 3, 5, 8, 13, 21, 34, 55, 89 .... etc.

Write a function call fib that has the function prototype:

```
int fib(int);
```

that will compute the nth Fibonacci number given the following rules:

fib(1) = 1, fib(2) = 1, fib(n) = fib(n-2) + fin(n-1)

3. Write and test a function called `computecircle()` that will compute both the area and circumference for a circle of given radius. It should have the following function prototype :-

```
void computecircle(float& a, float& c, float radius);
```

4. Write a program that contains a function to swap two integers. The function should have the following prototype:

```
void swap( int& a, int& b);
```

Chapter 8 (Week 3)

8.1 Program design notes

At some time in your course you will need to hand in an assignment which requires a little more documentation than a program listing and a couple of screen dumps. In these notes, we will be presenting the development of a single program - starting with a description of the problem and ending with a working program that has been tested.

Such an assignment may contain the following components:

1. **A statement of the problem** (or specification).

    In simple terms, you need to know what the project is about. If you choose your own assignment, it is up to you to provide the specification.

2. **An Analysis.**

    This is your interpretation of the problem. You are supposed to explain the problem in such a way, to show that you understand what is required, and suggest how it could be attempted. An analysis often involves research. You could look for similar problems and discuss how they relate to the problem that you have to solve.

3. **Design.**

    A design is a plan of how you are going to solve the problem. In this particular case, how you are going to write a C++ program.

    It is typically made up of a number of components such as:

    *   Design of Input. e.g. Screen layout and data entry
    *   Design of Output e.g. Output to screen and /or printer
    *   Data Storage
    *   Design of the program

4. **Implementation**

    This means writing the program and getting it to work. Proof of this stage is often satisfied by providing a listing of the program, and some of the output from the program in the form of a screen dump.

5. **Testing**

    The first criterion for testing a program is to ensure that it produces the correct results in all situations. This often involves providing test data to see if you get the results that you would expect to get. Another thing to consider is the ease of use to a user.

6.   **Evaluation of the System**

   Here you have to discuss your solution.

8.2 Specification

The following is an example of a problem that could be set for your coursework.

A local company wants to make a start at automating their payroll system. Currently the wage packets are made up individually. They get paid in cash and have a pay receipt that details hours worked, rate of pay, overtime and gross pay etc.

(a) Assuming a basic week is 37.5 hours and that any time over this is to be treated as overtime which is to be paid as 1.5 times the standard rate. Write a program that will accept input from the user for :-

   Employee name, hours worked, rate of pay

(b) The program will calculate :-

   overtime worked
   basic salary (not including overtime)
   overtime pay
   gross pay (basic salary + overtime pay)

(c) The program will display each of the values input from the keyboard, together with the items calculated above.

Add comments to document the program, and ensure that the program is readable by including appropriate indentation and spacing.

8.3 Analysis

This would appear to be a very simple program which requires the calculation of pay for a single employee. This could easily be computed using a calculator as follows:

Assume rate = 10.00 and hours = 45

basic pay = £37.5 × 10 = £375
overtime = 45 - 37.5 = 7.5   (hours worked - 37.5)
overtime pay = 7.5 × £10.00 × 1.5 = £112.50
gross pay = basic pay + overtime pay = £375.00 + £112.50 = 487.50

Here we assume that we have to subtract 37.5 from the number of hours worked to obtain the number of hours to be paid at the overtime rate. But what if the number of hours worked is less than 37·5.

We can conclude from this that if hours worked > 37.5 then there is overtime to be paid, otherwise there is no overtime.

There is a more difficult problem to resolve. If someone works less than the standard week (less that 37.5 hours) should they have their basic weekly pay reduced. The specification is not clear here - so it is open to interpretation.

We will be looking at the different interpretations that can be inferred from the specification. Version 1 takes the view that every employee will receive their basic weekly wage even if they work less than 37.5 hours.

8.4 Design

A program design usually starts with the programmer considering screen layout for input and output. The programming itself is usually very easy when you know where things are to appear on the screen. Plan it on paper first. Then write a few test programs to try out the layout. Do this for each of the screen layouts you intend to have in your program. Keep your screen designs and the program fragments that can generate such screens.

Another consideration is that of storage. In this program, we are only going to be using variables to store data. It is common practice to produce a table listing all variables. In this table you will describe the type of data that can be stored, and what it is going to be used for. Such a table is called a **data dictionary** by some. Programs using large amounts of data will probably use files. In this case, it will be necessary to design a **record structure**.

We are now in a position to start designing the program proper.

One method of designing a program is called **Top down Design** using a technique called **Stepwise Refinement**. The idea is to start with a very general description of the program. This description typically only has a few components. Then take each of these components in turn and provide more detail (add refinement). This often means that the components themselves get broken into smaller components, until such a time that the components are detailed enough that they can be translated into C++ code.

This design method can be represented using either **pseudo-code** or a more graphical, means such as **structure-charts**. A well known methodology that uses structure charts is called **Jackson Structured programming** (JSP). It was designed by Michael Jackson, but not the one who use to sing and dance, nor the Michael Jackson who is a world famous expert on beer.

1ˢᵗ level design (pseudocode)

1. Enter details
2. Perform calculations
3. Output results

Structure chart

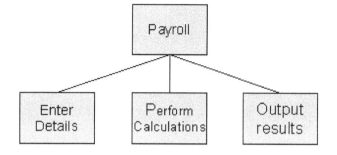

2ⁿᵈ level design

Enter details
1.1 Enter employees name
1.2 Enter number of hours worked
1.3 Enter hourly rate of pay

Perform calculations
2.1 Calculate overtime
2.2 Calculate basic pay
2.3 Calculate gross pay

Output results
3.1 Display Employee name
3.2 Display number of hours worked
3.3 Display Hourly rate of pay
3.4 Display Basic pay
3.5 Display number of hours overtime worked
3.6 Display overtime pay earned
3.7 Display gross pay

3ʳᵈ level design

This is to be done as a class exercise, and will include versions using pseudo-code and a structure chart (JSP).

Description of variables used

Variable name	Type	Description
empname	string	Employees name
hours	float	Number of hours worked
rate	float	Hourly rate of pay
overtime	float	number of hours overtime worked
basicpay	float	basic salary - not including overtime
overtimepay	float	overtime pay
grosspay	float	basic pay + overtime pay

8.5 Implementation

A program listing follows

Example 58

```cpp
//          Version 1 of Payroll program
#include <iostream>
#include <iomanip>
#include <string>
using namespace std;

int main()
{
    string name;
    float hours, rate;
    float overtime, basicpay, overtimepay, grosspay;

    // Enter employee details
    cout << "Enter name of employee : ";
    getline(cin, name);
    cout << "Enter number of hours worked : ";
    cin >> hours;
    cout << "Enter hourly rate of pay : ";
    cin >> rate;

    // Perform calculations
    if (hours > 37.5)
        overtime = hours - 37.5;
    else
        overtime = 0.0;

    basicpay = 37.5 * rate;

    overtimepay = overtime * 1.5 * rate;

    grosspay = basicpay + overtimepay;

    // Display all values
    cout << endl << endl;
    cout << fixed << setw(6) << setprecision(2);
    cout << "Employee name : " << name << endl;
    cout << "Hourly rate : " << rate << endl;
    cout << "basic pay = " << basicpay << "     ";
    cout << "overtime = " << overtime << "     ";
    cout << "overtimepay = " << overtimepay << endl;
    cout << "grosspay = " << grosspay << endl << endl;

    return 0;
}
```

Screen dump: Obtained by pressing the key 'Print Screen'. This was then pasted into Microsoft Paint. Paint can then be used to crop the image, so that just the relevant part is kept.

```
Enter name of employee : Tony Hawken
Enter number of hours worked : 17
Enter hourly rate of pay : 16.50


employee name : Tony Hawken
Number of hours worked : 17.00
Hourly rate : 16.50
basic pay = 618.75      overtime = 0.00      overtime pay =   0.00
grosspay = 618.75
```

Example 59

```cpp
//          Version 2 of Payroll program
//          Assumes that employees only get paid
//          for the hours that they work
#include <iostream>
#include <iomanip>
#include <string>
using namespace std;

int main()
{
    string name;
    float hours, rate;
    float overtime, basicpay, overtimepay, grosspay;

    // Enter employee details
    cout << "Enter name of employee : ";
    getline(cin, name);
    cout << "Enter number of hours worked : ";
    cin >> hours;
    cout << "Enter hourly rate of pay : ";
    cin >> rate;

    // Perform calculations
    if (hours > 37.5)
    {
        overtime = hours - 37.5;
        basicpay = rate * 37.5;

    }
    else
    {
        overtime = 0.0;
        basicpay = rate * hours;
```

```
    }
    overtimepay = overtime * rate * 1.5;
    grosspay = basicpay + overtimepay;

    // Display all values
    cout << endl << endl;
    cout << fixed << setw(6) << setprecision(2);
    cout << "Employee name : " << name << endl;
    cout << "Hourly rate : " << rate << endl;
    cout << "basic pay = " << basicpay << "     ";
    cout << "overtime = " << overtime << "     ";
    cout << "overtimepay = " << overtimepay << endl;
    cout << "grosspay = " << grosspay << endl << endl;

    return 0;
}
```

8.6 Demonstration of functions

There follows two further versions that are being used to demonstrate that there are different ways of doing things. There is also a brief description of each function. These are given as an example, as you will probably be asked for a description of all functions in your program, as part of your documentation.

8.6.1   Use a function to compute gross pay

Example 60

```
//         Version 3 of Payroll program
//         Uses a function to compute grosspay
#include <iostream>
#include <iomanip>
#include <string>

float grosspay(float, float);

int main()
{
    string name;
    float hours, rate;

    // Enter employee details
    cout << "Enter name of employee : ";
    getline(cin, name);
    cout << "Enter number of hours worked : ";
    cin >> hours;
    cout << "Enter hourly rate of pay : ";
    cin >> rate;
```

```
        cout << fixed << setw(6) << setprecision(2);
        cout << "grosspay = " << grosspay(hours, rate)
            << endl << endl;

        return 0;
}

float grosspay(float hours, float rate)
{
        float overtime, basicpay, overtimepay, grosspay;
        // Perform calculations
        if (hours > 37.5)
        {
                overtime = hours - 37.5;
                basicpay = rate * 37.5;
        }
        else
        {
                overtime = 0.0;
                basicpay = rate * hours;
        }
        overtimepay = overtime * rate * 1.5;
        grosspay = basicpay + overtimepay;
        return grosspay;
}
```

8.6.2   Description of the function `grosspay()`

The function `grosspay()` computes the amount of the gross pay given values for the number of hours worked and the hourly rate of pay. The function calculates the gross pay to be the sum of the basic pay and overtime pay. If more than 37.5 hours are worked, any extra time is deemed to be overtime. This is paid at a rate 1.5 times the hourly rate. The first 37.5 hours are paid at the normal rate. If less than 37.5 hours are worked, there is no overtime - then the gross pay is the number of hours worked times the hourly rate of pay.

8.6.3   Use a function to print a payslip

Example 61

```
// Version 4
// Includes a function to print a payslip

#include <iostream>
#include <iomanip>
#include <string>

void payslip(string, float, float);

int main()
```

```
{
    string name;
    float hours, rate;

    cout << "Enter name : ";
    getline(cin, name);
    cout << "Enter hours worked : ";
    cin >> hours;
    cout << "Enter hourly rate of pay : ";
    cin >> rate;
    payslip(name, hours, rate);
    return 0;
}

void payslip(string name, float hours, float rate)
{
    float overtime, basicpay, overtimepay, grosspay;

    if (hours > 37.5)
    {
        overtime = hours - 37.5;
        basicpay = 37.5 * rate;
    }
    else
    {
        basicpay = hours * rate;
        overtime = 0.0;
    }
    overtimepay = overtime * rate * 1.5;
    grosspay = basicpay + overtimepay;

    // Output results
    cout << setw(7) << setprecision(2) << endl << endl;
    cout << "name: " << name << endl;
    cout << "basic pay : " << basicpay << endl;
    cout << "overtime pay : " << overtimepay << endl;
    cout << "gross pay : " << grosspay << endl;
}
```

8.6.4   Description of the function `payslip()`

The function `payslip()` has no return value - any values that are computed are instead printed out. The function has four parameters - name, hours and rate. The parameter **name** is a string and stores the name of the employee to be printed on the payslip. The parameter **hours** represents the number of hours worked and **rate** represents the hourly rate of pay. The two parameters can be used to compute basic pay, overtime, overtime pay and gross pay. All of these values are then displayed by the function.

8.7 Testing

There are some things that you need to bear in mind, even for the most simple of assignments.

1. The program must work giving correct results.

    Check the results using a calculator and compare the results with those obtained using our program.

2. The Input part of the program must be easy to use

    Add additional prompts if necessary. But don't make them too complicated by including too much information.

3. The Output must be neat, easy to read and convey the correct information.

    This is often called acceptance testing. i.e. it must be acceptable to the customer who intends to use your program.

Debugging is the process of correcting errors that have been found while coding the program or by testing. It cannot occur unless you are aware of a program error.

Some of the errors (compilation errors) are easy to detect as they are due to incorrect syntax. In this case the location of where the error occurs is highlighted and it is accompanied by an error message that describes the error.

Other errors are accompanied by error messages and a probable location. This time it is not a question of logic, but having executed a forbidden action. An example of this is dividing by zero, or an out of bounds error caused by reading past the end of an array.

The most difficult to locate are logic errors. These errors don't necessarily produce error messages. They do however produce the wrong results.

There are many traditional techniques used by programmers to locate bugs in their programs. The simplest is to provide a **trace** in a portion of suspect code. In most cases this is achieved by addition of extra print statements which are used to dump the contents of all variables as they are updated. Also statements are used to display a message whenever a certain portion of code is executed. This is useful to ensure that part of the program can be reached.

The flow of a program, and the name of each procedure that gets called can be verified by including a **cout** statement within each statement that will display the name of the procedure each time it is called.

Termination of loops also need to be verified. Initially you may just want to display the number of iterations. In other situations you may need to check each iteration in detail to ascertain that both the action of the loop is carried out correctly and also that termination occurs correctly.

A manual variant of this is called a desk check or dry-run. This is achieved by filling in a blank table with the values of variables as they get updated.

Note: Dry-run's for the previous programs are left as an exercise.

8.8 Evaluation

The purpose of the evaluation is to provide a realistic appraisal of your program. It should reveal the weak points as well as areas where the program fulfils the user requirements. For each of the weak points try and suggest where and how improvements could be made.

The evaluation of this programming assignment is left as an exercise – Exercise 3-1

Exercise 8-1

1. Write a short user guide to explain how to use this program.

2. Describe any problems you have with entering data. Suggest how you can overcome these problems.

3. Produce a test plan to test the calculations performed by this program. You might consider producing a blank table, which you can then fill in with the aid of a pocket calculator. Then use this to compare with the results given by the program. Use several sets of data.

4. Produce several designs using both pseudo-code and JSP (structure chart) for this program. Start with a top-level design and then add to it - thus demonstration top-down design

8.9 Jackson Structured programming

In this chapter we will look at a particular program design methodology called Jackson Structured Programming or just JSP in short. This methodology uses structure charts and uses the principle of stepwise refinement. It also holds that all programs should be built from the three fundamental structured control-constructs – sequences, selection and iteration. The JSP structure charts are applicable to both data and programs. The structure charts for the data should show correspondences with the structure chart of the program that is to process this data.

We will start by looking at how the 3 basic control constructs are depicted using JSP.

Construct	JSP Structure chart	JSP pseudocode	program code

Sequence		A. <u>seq</u>
		   do B
		   do C
		   do D
		A. <u>end</u>
			B;
			C;
			D;

Selection		A. A. <u>select</u>
		       do B
		    A. <u>or</u>
		       do C
		    A. <u>end</u>
			if <condition>
			   B;
			else
			   C;
			
			if <condition>
			   B;

Iteration		A. <u>iter</u>
		   do B
		A. <u>end</u>
			while <cond>
			   B;

8.10 Example program design using JSP

Write a program to draw two types of box as illustrated below. Above the boxes, you will notice the required graphics characters and their respective ASCII codes.

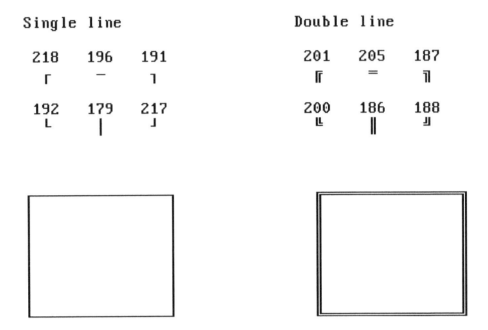

Extended ASCII characters required to draw boxes

Single line			Double line		
218	196	191	201	205	187
┌	─	┐	╔	=	╗
192	179	217	200	186	188
└	│	┘	╚	‖	╝

Press any key to continue

Using extended ASCII codes to draw boxes

We will produce a design to produce the double line box. An Initial design would probably look like this.

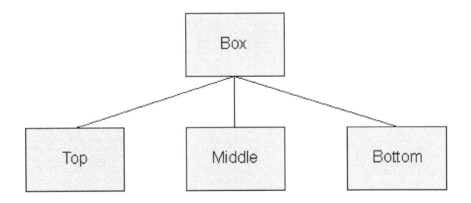

Initial design of a box

108

As it was stated before, JSP uses the idea of stepwise refinement. Now all we have to do is to expand the above design. We will start by examining how a first line of the box is composed. This we have called top.

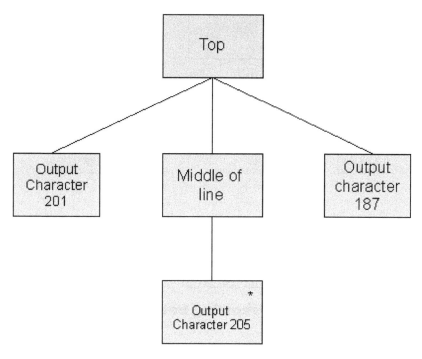

Design showing a refinement of top

The middle part of the box can be represented as follows:

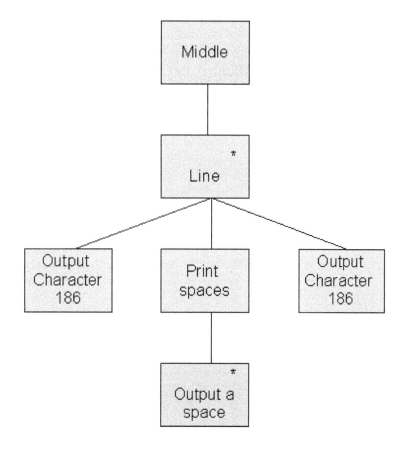

Design showing refinement of Middle

The second level design for bottom is similar to top. For completeness is included below.

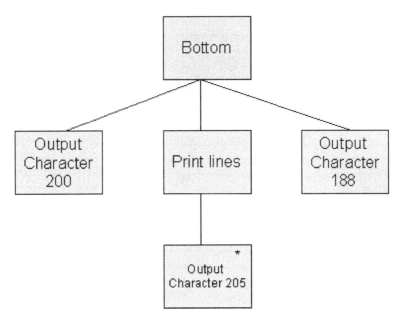

Design showing bottom

8.11 Implementation

You will notice that we now have sufficient detail to write the program. A program corresponding to the final design is as follows:

Example 62

```
#include <iostream>
using namespace std;

void drawbox(int, int);
void top(int);
void middle(int, int);
void bottom(int);

int main()
{
    drawbox(20, 8); // draw box 20 characters across,
                    // 8 lines down
    return 0;
}

void top(int x1)
{
    char ch = 201;
```

```cpp
        cout << ch;
        ch = 205;
        for (int x = 1; x <= x1; x++)
             cout << ch;
        ch = 187;
        cout << ch << endl;
}

void middle(int x1, int y1)
{
        char ch = 186;
        for(int y = 1; y <= y1-2; y++)
        {
             cout << ch;
             for(int x = 1; x <= x1; x++)
                  cout << " ";
             cout << ch << endl;
        }
}

void bottom(int x1)
{
        char ch = 200;
        cout << ch;
        ch = 205;
        for(int x = 1; x <= x1; x++)
             cout << ch;
        ch = 188;
        cout << ch;
}

void drawbox(int x, int y)
{
        top(x);
        middle(x,y);
        bottom(x);
}
```

Chapter 9 (week 9)

An example coursework (A typical assignment)

9.1 Module 2 Assignment (Specification)

Assignment for module 2

In the last year or two, many banks have been bailed out by the taxpayer. It is thought that one of the reasons for their failure is their bonus culture.

A survey is to be conducted, which will collect responses to the statement "All bonuses to bank employees should be banned".

You are required to use the above information in the assignment.

Program

(a) Write a function that will display the above information and will also provide a menu of choices for the user to respond. The menu should include the following choices.

1. Strongly agree
2. Agree
3. Don't know
4. Disagree
5. Strongly disagree
6. Quit menu

(b) Write a driver program to test this function. This program should include the function `main()` and anything else to test this function. Save this as Ass2b

(c) To your driver program, add another function. This function will allow a user to enter a number representing their choice. It should also be able to update variables that are to be used to maintain a count of how many people vote for each choice. Save this as Ass2c

(d) Modify this driver program (Ass2c), so that will include appropriate control structures that will allow at least 10 people to use the program and record their opinion. Save this as Ass2d.

(e) Add another function that will display the results of the survey in the form of a neat table. Save this as Ass2e. Make sure that this version of the program is clearly laid out, has consistent indentation and that there are appropriate comments to document the program.

Documentation required

Produce a word-processed document of at least 5 pages that will include the following.

Analysis – a description of what you expect the program to do, and how you expect to implement the program.

Program design – A structure chart to illustrate the overall design of the program. In particular, the relationship between the main program and functions used must be shown. Pseudo-code can also be used to describe the functions.

Functions used – a concise description of each procedure should be included.

Program listing – the program should include appropriate comments and easy to read.

Screen dumps – at least two screen dumps should be included. One to show the appearance of the questions and input, the second to show the final results in the form of a table.

Evaluation – this should include a description of any problems you had and your opinion of the suitability of the program. You could also include the reason you did it the way you did.

9.2 Driver program and function (Ass2b)

The reason for writing single functions and testing them first rather than write a whole program from scratch, is that is far easier to test for and spot errors. This is a common technique employed by programmers. It is also a technique that I advise you to employ, as you will be able to complete your coursework much quicker if you attempt a part of the program at a time in this manner. When you are satisfied that this function works, it is an easy matter to include another function and proceed in the same manner.

This part of the program was easily achievable without having to think about design.

<u>Example 63</u>

```cpp
//Simple driver program
#include <iostream>

using namespace std;

void menu(void);

int main()
{
    menu();

    return 0;
}

void menu(void)
{
    cout << "Survey" << endl << endl;
    cout << "In the last year or two many British banks have"
        << " been bailed out" << endl;
    cout << "by the taxpayer. It is thought that one of the"
        << " reasons for their" << endl;
    cout << "failure is their bonus culture." << endl << endl;
    cout << "Answer the following statement with a response 1-5"
        << endl;
    cout << "All bonuses to bank employees should be banned"
        << endl << endl;

    cout << "\t1.\tStrongly agree\n";
    cout << "\t2.\tAgree\n";
    cout << "\t3.\tDon\'t know\n";
    cout << "\t4.\tDisagree\n";
    cout << "\t5.\tStrongly agree\n";
    cout << "\t6.\tQuit menu\n\n";
}
```

```
C-\ Quincy 2005                                                    - □ ×
Survey                                                              ▲

In the last year or two many British banks have been bailed out
by the taxpayer. It is thought that one of the reasons for their
failure is their bonus culture.

Answer the following statement with a response 1-5
All bonuses to bank employees should be banned

        1.          Strongly agree
        2.          Agree
        3.          Don't know
        4.          Disagree
        5.          Strongly agree
        6.          Quit menu


Press Enter to return to Quincy...
```

Screen dump for ass2b

9.3 Analysis

The way the program has been specified, it is quite clear how the program could be structured, as the main functions have already been specified.

Starting with these, for the first function mentioned we are required to display the nature of the survey and the choices that are to be presented to each user. This is extremely easy, as no variables are required, and no parameters need to be passed. There is no return value for this function as we are merely displaying something and not calculating a value.

The function to enter a choice is more difficult. Here we need to pass a variable – a value indicating the users choice. Although the value is entered within the function we need to have a copy of this value, as it is to be used as a data terminator as well. The last option on the menu – 6 is used as a data terminator. We can then test for this value to terminate the loop, indicating that everyone has used the program and completed the survey.

The main purpose of this function however, is to perform a count of votes for each option. For this to occur, we need to have 5 variables to record the count. Each time someone votes for a particular option, the corresponding variable is incremented by 1. In this implementation the variables used to count the votes have been made global, making it easy to access them.

A while loop is used to test for the value 6. When found, the loop will terminate. Each time the loop repeats, the menu options need to be displayed and the ability to enter you option needs to be present. Rather than allow all the output to scroll down the screen – which could appear very messy, it was decided that the screen would be cleared each time. That way fresh output would appear at the top of the screen.

9.4 Design (ass2e)

The structure chart below indicates the overall design. A more detailed design could have been given for the underlying functions. Pseudo code is a good means to describe the design for these.

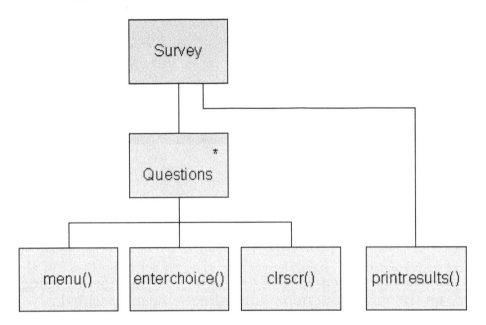

Structure chart for ass2e

9.5 Final program (ass2e)

The program listing and a screen dump for ass2e follows.

Example 64

```
#include <iostream>
#include <conio2.h>        //required for clrscr()

using namespace std;

void menu(void);
void enterchoice(int&);
void printresults(void);

//global variables - maintain count
int c1 = 0, c2 = 0, c3 = 0, c4 = 0, c5 = 0;

int main()
{
     int ch = 0;
     //Display and answer questions
     while (ch != 6)
     {
          menu();
```

116

```cpp
        enterchoice(ch);
        clrscr();        //clear screen after each user
    }

    printresults();
    return 0;
}


//Display statement and menu choices
void menu(void)
{
    cout << "Survey" << endl << endl;
    cout << "In the last year or two, many British banks have"
        << " been bailed out" << endl;
    cout << "by the taxpayer. It is thought that one of the"
        << " reasons for their" << endl;
    cout << "failure is their bonus culture." << endl << endl;
    cout << "Answer the following statement with a response 1-5"
        << endl;
    cout << "All bonuses to bank employees should be banned"
        << endl << endl;
    cout << "\t1.\tStrongly agree\n";
    cout << "\t2.\tAgree\n";
    cout << "\t3.\tDon\'t know\n";
    cout << "\t4.\tDisagree\n";
    cout << "\t5.\tStrongly agree\n";
    cout << "\t6.\tQuit menu\n\n";
}


// Enter a choice 1-5, 6 to quit and increment corresponding count
// variable
void enterchoice(int& ch)
{
    cout << "Enter 1-6 to indicate your opinion : ";
    cin >> ch;

    switch(ch)
    {
        case 1:    c1++; break;
        case 2:    c2++; break;
        case 3:    c3++; break;
        case 4:    c4++; break;
        case 5:    c5++; break;
        case 6:    break;
        default:   cout << "Invalid choice - Enter 1 to 6";
    }
}


// Display results of survey by printing values of the counters
// c1 - c5
void printresults(void)
{
```

117

```cpp
    cout << "Results of the survey are as follows : \n\n";
    cout << "\t1.\tstrongly agree\t\t" << c1 << endl;
    cout << "\t2.\tAgree\t\t\t" << c2 << endl;
    cout << "\t3.\tDon\'t know\t\t" << c3 << endl;
    cout << "\t4.\tDisagree\t\t" << c4 << endl;
    cout << "\t5.\tStrongly disagree\t" << c5 << endl << endl;
}
```

```
Quincy 2005                                                    _ □ ✕
Results of the survey are as follows :

        1.      strongly agree          6
        2.      Agree                   8
        3.      Don't know              3
        4.      Disagree                1
        5.      Strongly disagree       1


Press Enter to return to Quincy..._
```

Screen dump to show results table

9.6 Linking (ass2e)

The library conio2.h provides the programmer with a Borland-style implementation of console input and output. In particular we wish to use the clrscr() function to clear the screen after each user has entered their choice.

Because this is an external library to the compiler, we need to change the linkage options to ensure that the necessary code is linked into our program. It is not enough to just include the directive #include <conio.h>, as this only contains the prototypes to use the functions.

In particular, **-lconio** needs to be added to the Linker options.

To obtain these options, you must first click on **Tools**, then **Options**.

Now when you compile and link your program, there will be no errors as all the necessary components of the program will be in place.

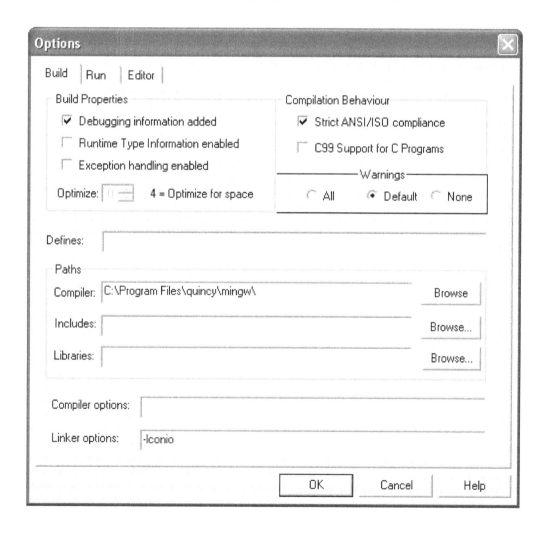

9.7 Evaluation

The program satisfies the specification, in that everything that has been asked for has been achieved. A data terminator together with a while loop to check for this value enables you to run this program as many times as you like. There is nothing to stop you however looping less than 10 times if you choose to terminate the loop earlier.

The functions in the program each have a clear and simple function to achieve, and they do what is required under normal circumstances. The main problem is with the function enterchoice(). There is no problem if a number is entered, as there is a test within the switch statement for numbers not in the range 1-6. But, if anything else is entered the program is liable to crash.

Another problem, is that global variables are used. This is generally considered to be bad programming practice. For this reason, another version of the program follows, that avoids this problem. That is the variables are passed by reference so that they can be updated by enterchoice().

9.8 Another version of final program

Example 65

```
#include <iostream>
#include <conio2.h> //required for clrscr()

using namespace std;

void menu(void);
void enterchoice(int&, int&, int&, int&, int&, int&);
void printresults(int, int, int, int, int);

int main()
{
    int ch = 0;     // Current choice entered
    //variables to count votes
    int c1 = 0, c2 = 0, c3 = 0, c4 = 0, c5 = 0;
    while (ch != 6)
    {
        menu();
        enterchoice(ch, c1, c2, c3, c4, c5);
        clrscr();
    }

    printresults(c1, c2, c3, c4, c5);
    return 0;
}

void menu(void)
{
```

```cpp
        cout << "Survey" << endl << endl;
        cout << "In the last year or two many British banks have"
                << " been bailed out" << endl;
        cout << "by the taxpayer. It is thought that one of the"
                << " reasons for their" << endl;
        cout << "failure is their bonus culture." << endl << endl;
        cout << "Answer the following statement with a response 1-5"
                << endl;
        cout << "All bonuses to bank employees should be banned"
                << endl << endl;


        cout << "\t1.\tStrongly agree\n";
        cout << "\t2.\tAgree\n";
        cout << "\t3.\tDon\'t know\n";
        cout << "\t4.\tDisagree\n";
        cout << "\t5.\tStrongly agree\n";
        cout << "\t6.\tQuit menu\n\n";
}

// Enter a choice 1-5, 6 to quit. Increment corresponding count
variable
void enterchoice(int& ch,
                 int &ch1, int &ch2, int &ch3, int &ch4, int &ch)
{
        cout << "Enter 1-6 to indicate your opinion : ";
        cin >> ch;

        switch(ch)
        {
                case 1:         ch1++; break;
                case 2:         ch2++; break;
                case 3:         ch3++; break;
                case 4:         ch4++; break;
                case 5:         ch5++; break;
                case 6:         break;
                default:  cout << "Invalid choice - Enter 1 to 6";
        }
}


// Display results of survey by printing values of the
// counters c1 - c5
void printresults(int c1, int c2, int c3, int c4, int c5)
{
        cout << "Results of the survey are as follows : \n\n";
        cout << "\t1.\tstrongly agree\t\t" << c1 << endl;
        cout << "\t2.\tAgree\t\t\t" << c2 << endl;
        cout << "\t3.\tDon\'t know\t\t" << c3 << endl;
        cout << "\t4.\tDisagree\t\t" << c4 << endl;
        cout << "\t5.\tStrongly disagree\t" << c5 << endl << endl;
}
```

Chapter 10 (week 10)

10.1   Tasks to do

This week is to be devoted to finishing the programming assignment. You should have another look at chapter 5 – to remind yourself of what needs to be done. Also refer back to the previous chapter.

You will notice that there is much more emphasis on design and that there is more demands about the documentation required. In particular a structure chart (JSP) is required for the final program.

10.2   End of unit summary

1. The for statement is used to repeat code a fixed number of times. It employs a control variable that is used as a counter.

2. A while loop is used when we don't know in advance how many times we want to repeat a certain section of code. The terminating condition appears at the top of the loop and typically tests for a certain value.

3. A do... while loop is similar to a while loop, except that the loop-terminating condition comes at the end of the loop.

4. The best way to write and maintain a large program, is to split up the program into smaller components. The program code in these smaller components can be stored in functions, which can be activated by a function call.

5. A program that uses functions will for each function, have a function declaration or prototype, a function definition and one or more function calls.

6. A function prototype has the same format as the function header of the function definition. It is used by the compiler to match the parameters and return value type.

7. The function definition is where you specify the actions of the function.

8. The function call, executes the function. If there are any parameters, these are passed to the body of the function and the values passed are stored as local variables.

9. When the function has finished executing the program returns to the part of the program where the function was called. The function call also usually accepts the return value. Either it is stored in a variable or printed out.

10. A recursive function is a function that is self-referential – that is it refers to itself. When you write a recursive function, it does one of two things, it either calls itself or terminates.

11. A program is a specific type of algorithm that you can run on your computer. Another form of algorithm is pseudo-code. Pseudo-code is used in program design, as it can be used to specify what you want your program to do. An algorithm written in the form of pseudo-code can be used to write a program in any language you choose.

12. A structure chart is a graphical representation. Jackson Structure Programming (JSP) is a particular design methodology that uses structure charts. JSP uses the three constructs that represent structured programming – sequence, selection and repetition.

part 3

Arrays, structures and text file processing

Aims

After completing this 5-week unit, you will be able to do the following:

Arrays

Declare an array, assign values to it and use a loop to process the contents of an array. Be able to solve a variety of problems using arrays

Write functions that can process arrays. Pass an Array as a parameter to a function

Structures

Declare a struct to create a record structure and create objects of this type.

Be able to access elements in a record structure.

Create an array of records and be able to process it.

Files

Create file stream operators to open a file, write data to a file and read data from a file.

Be able to test for success of opening a file, and detect the end-of-file.

Write a program that uses files for a particular purpose.

Chapter 11 (Week 11)

11.1   Arrays

When processing large amounts of similar data, it makes sense if we can treat this data as a whole. Then we can easily repeat the same operation on the data.

A collection of like data items is called an array. These can be created in C++ as follows:

```
int numbers[10];      // Array to store 10 integers
char name[20];        // Array to store 20 characters
```

All we need to know in advance is how many elements we intend to store in the array.

Individual elements of an array are accessed by reference to an **index**. An index is merely a number that refers to the position within an array. In C++ the first element has the index 0. Because we can refer to each element in turn using its index, it is very easy to use a for loop to process the data in an array, making use of the control variable within the for loop to identify the item of data to be processed.

One dimensional arrays or lists can be used to model simple situations where a large stream of data is to be used.

Two dimensional arrays or tables can be used to model such things as multiplication tables, board games such as chess or battleships, the computer screen if we wish to plot some graphics.

Arrays are important in many areas of computing. They can be used to store data that we can then sort, or search for an item of interest.

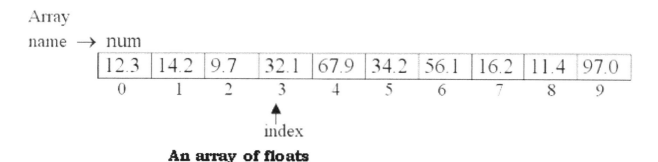

An array of floats

The above array can be declared as follows:

```
float num[10];
```

A value can be stored into any chosen position by assignment

```
num[3] = 32.1
```

125

Question: What is the 6th element of the above? How could you display it using C++?

11.2 Example programs using arrays

Example 65

```cpp
#include <iostream>
using namespace std;

int main()
{
    int dice[] = {1, 2, 3, 4, 5, 6};
    for(int c = 0; c < 6; c++)
        cout << "dice[" << c << "] = " << dice[c] << endl;
    return 0;
}
```

```
C:\Program Files\quincy\bin\quincy.exe          _ □ ×
dice[0] = 1
dice[1] = 2
dice[2] = 3
dice[3] = 4
dice[4] = 5
dice[5] = 6

Press Enter to return to Quincy...
```

Notes:

1. The statement `int dice[] = {1, 2, 3, 4, 5, 6};` defines an array with the initial values 1, 2, 3, 4, 5, 6.

2. There is no need to specify the number of elements in the array as there is a set of 6 numbers to initialise the array.

The following program illustrates many features of arrays, such as: storing elements, displaying the contents of an array, finding the total sum of all the elements and displaying the smallest value.

Example 66

```cpp
#include <iostream>
#include <iomanip>
using namespace std;

int main()
{
    float a[10];          // An array of 10 floats

    // Store 10 numbers entered from keyboard
    for(int c = 0; c < 10; c++)
```

126

```
        {
            cout << "Enter next number : ";
            cin >> a[c];
        }

        cout << fixed << setprecision(2);    // 2 decimal places

        // Display contents of array
        for(c = 0; c < 10; c++)
            cout << "a[" << c << "] = " << a[c] << endl;

        // Sum elements of the array
        float total = 0.0;  // Declare and initialize total
        for(c = 0; c < 10; c++)
            total += a[c];
        cout << "Sum of elements = " << total << endl;

        // Display smallest element
        float min = a[0];    // Start with first element as minimum
        for(c = 1; c < 10; c++)
            if(a[c] < min)
                min = a[c];
        cout << "Smallest number is " << min << endl;
        return 0;
}
```

```
Quincy 2005                                                    _ □ ×
Enter next number : 4
Enter next number : 5
Enter next number : 6
Enter next number : 7
Enter next number : 3
Enter next number : 6
Enter next number : 6
Enter next number : 7
Enter next number : 8
Enter next number : 6
a[0] = 4
a[1] = 5
a[2] = 6
a[3] = 7
a[4] = 3
a[5] = 6
a[6] = 6
a[7] = 7
a[8] = 8
a[9] = 6
Sum of elements = 58
Smallest number is 3

Press Enter to return to Quincy..._
```

Notes:

The $(c+1)^{th}$ element is accessed using `a[c]`.

11.3   C-strings

This example illustrates character strings. Before the string class came about, this was the most common way of creating and manipulating strings. They are now often referred to as C-strings.

Example 67

```cpp
#include <iostream>
#include <cstring>
using namespace standard;

int main()
{
    char s1[] = "Tony";
    char s2[] = {'H', 'a', 'w', 'k', 'e', 'n', '\0'};
    char s3[20];
    cout << "s1 = " << s1 << endl;
    cout << "The third character of s1 is " << s1[2] << endl;
    cout << "The length of s1 is " << strlen(s1) << endl;
    cout << "s2 = " << s2 << endl;
    cout << "s2 with the first 3 characters removed is ";
    cout << s2 + 3 << endl;
    cout << "The length of s2 is " << strlen(s2) << endl;
    strcpy(s3, s1);
    cout << "s3 = " << s3 << endl;
    strcpy(s3 + 4, " ");
    strcpy(s3 + 5, s2);
    cout << "s3 = " << s3 << endl;
    return 0;
}
```

```
CN  Quincy 2005                                            _ □ ✕
s1 = Tony
The third character of s1 is n
The length of s1 is 4
s2 = Hawken
s2 with the first 3 characters removed is ken
The length of s2 is 6
s3 = Tony
s3 = Tony Hawken

Press Enter to return to Quincy..._
```

Notes:

1. You can initialise a c-string by assigning it to a list of characters. The c-string s2 is initialised in this manner.

2. You can specify a fixed length for a c-string. See s3.

3. The function call `strcpy(s3, s1)` copies s1 to s3.

11.4   Using functions to process arrays

In this example we will be using arrays to store statistics, and then using a small collection of functions to compute the mean, variance and standard deviation. The table below is a grouped frequency table representing marks scored in a small FE college.

Mark	Frequency
1 - 20	8
21 - 30	30
31 - 40	90
41 - 50	103
51 - 60	79
61 - 70	64
71 - 80	21
81 - 90	5

$$\text{Mean} = \frac{\Sigma fx}{\Sigma f} = \mu$$

$$\text{Variance} = \frac{\Sigma fx^2}{\Sigma f} - \mu^2 = \sigma^2$$

$$\text{Standard deviation} = \sqrt{\sigma^2} = \sigma$$

To use the above statistics we have evaluated a mid-mark **x**. This we can use to calculate estimates for the mean, variance and standard deviation.

<u>Example 68</u>

```cpp
#include <iostream>
#include <cmath>
using namespace std;

void getdata(float [], int [], int);
float sumfx(float [], int [], int);
int sumf(int f[], int);
float sumfx2(float [], int [], int);
void displaydata(float [], int [], int);

int main()
{
    float x[20];
    int f[20];
    int n;
    cout << "Enter number of items in each array : ";
    cin >> n;
    getdata(x, f, n); // enter data

    // Statistical calculations
    float mean = sumfx(x, f, n) / sumf(f, n);
    float variance = sumfx2(x, f, n) / sumf(f, n) - mean * mean;
    float sd = sqrt(variance);

    // Output results
    displaydata(x, f, n);
    cout << "Mean = " << mean << endl;
    cout << "Variance = " << variance << endl;
    cout << "Standard deviation = " << sd << endl;
```

```cpp
        return 0;
}

void getdata(float x[], int f[], int n)
{
    int lm, hm;
    for(int c = 0; c < n; c++)
    {
        cout << "Entering data for group " << (c + 1) << endl;
        cout << "Enter lowest mark : ";
        cin >> lm;
        cout << "Enter highest mark : ";
        cin >> hm;
        x[c] = (float) (lm + hm) / 2;
        cout << "Enter frequency : ";
        cin >> f[c];
    }
}

float sumfx(float x[], int f[], int n)
{
    float sum = 0.0;
    for (int c = 0; c < n; c++)
        sum += f[c] * x[c];
    return sum;
}

int sumf(int f[], int n)
{
    int sum = 0;
    for(int c = 0; c < n; c++)
        sum += f[c];
    return sum;
}

float sumfx2(float x[], int f[], int n)
{
    float sum = 0.0;
    for(int c = 0; c < n; c++)
        sum += f[c] * x[c] * x[c];
    return sum;
}

void displaydata(float x[], int f[], int n)
{
    cout << "x\tf\n";
    for(int c = 0; c < n; c++)
        cout << x[c] << "\t" << f[c] << endl;
}
```

```
Enter number of items in each array : 5
Entering data for group 1
Enter lowest mark : 1
Enter highest mark : 5
Enter frequency : 2
Entering data for group 2
Enter lowest mark : 6
Enter highest mark : 10
Enter frequency : 4
Entering data for group 3
Enter lowest mark : 11
Enter highest mark : 15
Enter frequency : 5
Entering data for group 4
Enter lowest mark : 16
Enter highest mark : 20
Enter frequency : 4
Entering data for group 5
Enter lowest mark : 21
Enter highest mark : 25
Enter frequency : 1
x       f
3       2
8       4
13      5
18      4
23      1
Mean = 12.375
Variance = 30.8594
Standard deviation = 5.55512

Press Enter to return to Quincy..._
```

Notes:

1. An entire array can be passed to a function, by passing the name of the array as a parameter. A reference is not needed because the name of an array is a reference to a memory address where the array starts.

2. The prototype **void getdata(float [], int [], int);** lists 3 parameters. The first is an array of type float. The second is an array of type int, and the third is an integer.

3. The function call **getdata(x, f, n);** passes the actual parameters x, f and n. Here x is an array of floats, x is an array of integers, and n is an integer.

Exercise 11-1

1. Write a program that will:

   (a) generate 100 random numbers in the range 1 - 100 and store them in an array.

   (b) calculate and display the minimum, maximum, average of all numbers stored in the array.

2. Write a program that will:

   (a) allow you to enter a number indicating how many Strings you wish to enter at the keyboard

   (b) create an array for storing exactly the number of Strings that you wish

   (c) print out each String in the array together with the length of the string

   (d) compute and print out the average length of the strings entered.

3. Write a program that will convert a Roman number to decimal. The user should be prompted to enter a Roman number, and this should be stored in a string.

Notes: (Q1)

1. You will need to use two functions :

   ```
   int random(int n);   //return an integer in the range 0 to n-1
   void srand(void);    // randomize first random number
   ```

2. You will need the header files <cstdlib> to use these.

Notes: (Q3)

1. Use an array of integers to store the decimal equivalent of each character of the Roman number. It is then much easier to compute the total decimal number.

2. As a reminder valid Roman numerals are as follows:

Roman numeral:	I	V	X	L	C	D	M
Decimal equivalent:	1	5	10	50	100	500	1000

11.5   Searching and Sorting

In this section we are going to look at some more advanced applications of arrays. This will give you an introduction to the topic of searching and sorting data.

The simplest type of searching technique is called a **Linear Search**. In simple terms this means starting at the beginning of an array and scanning the array one element at a time until the required item is found. The main loop to access the array might look like this:

```
int i = 0;
while ( i < 10 && num[i] != x)
    i++        // Skip past unwanted items
```

We now need to test which of the two conditions terminated the loop.

```
if (num[i] == x)
    cout <<"Item found at location " + << i << endl;
else
    cout << "Item not found" << endl;
```

This is an effective method to search for items in an array if the array is very small. But for large arrays it would be very slow as the number of comparisons and hence the time taken is proportional to the number of elements in the array.

Example 69

```
#include <iostream>
using namespace std;

int lsearch(int [], int, int);

int main()
{
    int num, result;
    int numbers[10] = {33, 42, 23, 76, 45, 32, 27, 23, 49, 22};
    cout << "Enter a number to search for: ";
    cin >> num;
    result = lsearch(numbers, 10, num);
    if(result != -1)
        cout << num << " was found at position "
            << result << endl;
    else
        cout << num << " was not found" << endl;
    return 0;
}

int lsearch(int a[], int n, int x)
{
    int i = 0;
    while(i < n and a[i] != x)
        i++; // Skip unwanted items
```

```
    if(a[i] == x)
        return i;
    else
        return -1;        // Indicate failure
}
```

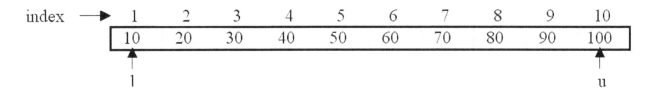

A faster method to search for an item in an array is called a Bisection Search. For this to work the items in the array must be sorted.

index ►	1	2	3	4	5	6	7	8	9	10
	10	20	30	40	50	60	70	80	90	100

1   u

The algorithm goes as follows:

Guess where the number is by selecting the middle element. The midpoint can be determined by midpt = (1 + u) / 2 . If we perform an integer division it doesn't matter whether we start with an even number or odd number of elements. In this case our initial mid-point will be element 5. We now have 3 possibilities:

1.   `number == num[midpt]      // Element is found.`

2.   `number < num[midpt]       //  Search left sublist`

3.   `number > num[midpt] // Search right sublist`

In this case condition 2 applies so we want to search the left sublist.

To do this set u = midpt - 1

Bisection search after initial comparison

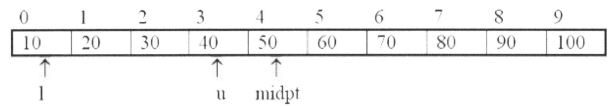

The new mid point can now be calculated with the expression `[1 + u] / 2` which gives us the value 2. A comparison of `num[midpt]` is made to see whether the element is found etc. This is repeated until either the desired data item is found or u > l.

Sorting is much more complicated than searching and involves many more comparisons. For this reason we will look at the simplest of sorts and leave a more detailed analysis until later. The simplest sort is the **bubble sort**. It contains two components, comparison and interchange. Adjacent elements of an array are compared to see if they are in the correct relative position. If not, they must be swapped round.

A strategy for doing that is as follows:

```
if(a[j] < a[j-1])
{
    int temp = a[j];
    a[j] = a[j-1];
    a[j-1] = temp;
}
```

Now a systematic means of ensuring that all elements are compared is required. A bubble sort compares adjacent elements for the entire array, swapping elements that are out of place 1 at a time.

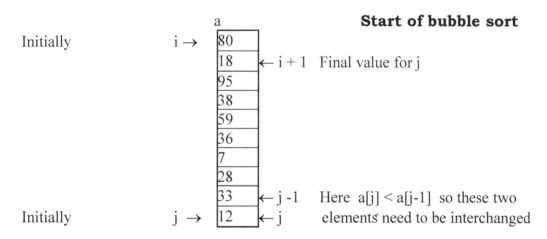

Start of bubble sort

Initially   i →   80
             18   ← i + 1   Final value for j
             95
             38
             59
             36
             7
             28
             33   ← j -1   Here a[j] < a[j-1] so these two
Initially   j →   12   ← j   elements need to be interchanged

Looking at the previous figure you will see for the first iteration j points to the last element and i to the first. Two elements a[j] and a[j-1] will be compared to see if they are in the correct place. The index j will continually be decremented until it takes a value i+1. Each time adjacent elements will get compared and will be swapped if they are in the wrong order. The complete method for performing a bubble sort should then look like this.

Example 70

```
#include <iostream>
using namespace std;

void bsort(int [], int);
void displaynumbers(int [], int);

int main()
{
    int numbers[20] = {37, 34, 87, 35, 86, 45, 6, 8, 43, 11,
                       99, 76, 65, 87, 45, 34, 21, 18, 85, 9};
    displaynumbers(numbers, 20);
```

135

```
        bsort(numbers, 20);
        displaynumbers(numbers, 20);

        return 0;
}

void bsort(int a[], int n)
{
        for(int i = 0; i < n; i++)
            for(int j = n-1; j > i; j--)
                if(a[j] < a[j-1])
                {
                        int temp = a[j];
                        a[j] = a[j-1];
                        a[j-1] = temp;
                }
}

void displaynumbers(int a[], int n)
{
        for(int i = 0; i < n; i++)
        cout << a[i] << "\t";
        cout << endl << endl;
}
```

```
Quincy 2005                                                                    _ □ ✕
37      34      87      35      86      45      6       8       43      11
99      76      65      87      45      34      21      18      85      9

6       8       9       11      18      21      34      34      35      37
43      45      45      65      76      85      86      87      87      99

Press Enter to return to Quincy...
```

11.6 Two dimensional arrays

A two dimensional array is sometimes called a table. A two dimensional array has two subscripts instead of one. It is a very common structure in everyday life. Objects like chess-boards, the screen of your monitor made up of pixels, and maps all have a tabular structure, and hence can be represented using two-dimensional arrays. The simplest is possibly the multiplication table.

The following code demonstrates the use of 2-dimensional arrays:

×	1	2	3	4	5	6	7	8	9	10
1	1	2	3	4	5	6	7	8	9	10
2	2	4	6	8	10	12	14	16	18	20
3	3	6	9	12	15	18	21	24	27	30
4	4	8	12	16	20	24	28	32	36	40
5	5	10	15	20	25	30	35	40	45	50
6	6	12	18	24	30	36	42	48	54	60
7	7	14	21	28	35	42	49	56	63	70
8	8	16	24	32	40	48	56	64	72	80
9	9	18	27	36	45	54	63	72	81	90
10	10	20	30	40	50	60	70	80	90	100

(col → across the top; row → down the left side)

Example 71

```cpp
#include <iostream>
#include <iomanip>
using namespace std;

int main()
{
    int table [10][10];

    for(int row = 0; row < 10; row++)
        for(int col = 0; col < 10; col++)
            table[row][col] = (row + 1) * (col + 1);


    // Print the table
    for(int row = 0; row < 10; row++)
    {
        for(int col = 0; col < 10; col++)
            cout << setw(5) << table[row][col];
        cout << endl;
    }

    return 0;
```

}

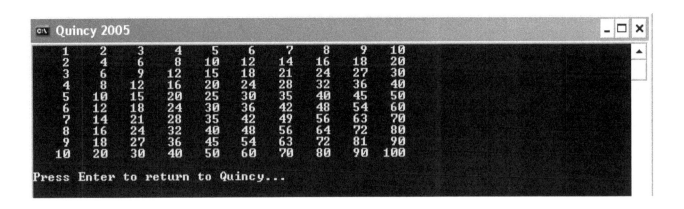

```
        1       2       3       4       5       6       7       8       9      10
        2       4       6       8      10      12      14      16      18      20
        3       6       9      12      15      18      21      24      27      30
        4       8      12      16      20      24      28      32      36      40
        5      10      15      20      25      30      35      40      45      50
        6      12      18      24      30      36      42      48      54      60
        7      14      21      28      35      42      49      56      63      70
        8      16      24      32      40      48      56      64      72      80
        9      18      27      36      45      54      63      72      81      90
       10      20      30      40      50      60      70      80      90     100

Press Enter to return to Quincy...
```

Exercise 11-2

1. Write a program which will:

   (a) Create an array called list capable of holding 20 numbers.

   (b) Populate this array using random numbers in the range 1 to 50.

   (c) Sort the array called list with a bubble sort.

   (d) Search for one of the numbers using a bisection search.

Chapter 12 (Week 12)

12.1 Structures in C++

Instead of using only individual variables to name each item of data we can group variables together to form a **structure**. In both the C and C++ language this can be done using the keyword struct.

```
struct person
{
    char name[20];
    float height;   // height in metres
    float weight;   // weight in Kg
};
```

The above code declares a new data type called person, made up of the variables name, height and weight. This declaration as it is called does not declare a variable, it just describes a new data type that is made up of a 20 character string, followed by 2 floats.

To declare a variable you have to use this new data type as follows:

```
person p1;
```

The above statement creates a variable called p1 that has enough storage allocated to store a 20 character string followed by 2 floats.

The member-data or fields as they are often called can be identified using a special dot notation

p1.name   refers to the **member data** called name within the object called p1.

You can use this to store values by assignment or any other method that you are familiar with. You can also access the current value by using cout to print it on the screen.

12.2 Example programs using structures

There follows 7 complete example programs to indicate how structures can be used.

Example 72

```cpp
#include <iostream>
#include <iomanip>
using namespace std;

struct person
{
    char name[20];
    float height;  // height in metres
    float weight;  // weight in Kg
};

int main()
{
    person p1;      // Create an object of type person
    cout << "Enter name : ";
    cin.getline(p1.name, 20);
    cout << "Enter height in metres : ";
    cin >> p1.height;
    cout << "Enter weight in Kg : ";
    cin >> p1.weight;

    // Display contents of p1
    cout << "Name" << "\t\t" << "height (m)"
        << "\t" << "weight (Kg)\n";
    cout << p1.name << "\t" << p1.height
        << "\t\t" << p1.weight << endl;

    // Calculate and display weight to height ratio
    float ratio = p1.weight / p1.height;
    cout << fixed << setprecision(2) << "Ratio = "
        << ratio << endl;

    return 0;
}
```

```
Quincy 2005                                            _ □ ×
Enter name : Tony Hawken
Enter height in metres : 1.75
Enter weight in Kg : 76
Name            height (m)      weight (Kg)
Tony Hawken     1.75            76
Ratio = 43

Press Enter to return to Quincy..._
```

Notes:

1. The keyword **struct** is used to group data or create a record structure.

2. Name, height and weight can be considered to be fields in a record. Often referred to as **member data**.

3. The **struct** definition is used to create a new data type.

4. The statement   person p;   is used to create a data item or object of type person.

5. p1.name   refers to the field called name within the **object** p1. Member data in a struct can always be accessed in this manner.

6. This form of the getline() function is used, because we are using a c-string rather than a string object.

```
cin.getline(p1.name, 20);
```

Example 73

```cpp
#include <iostream>
#include <iomanip>
using namespace std;

struct person
{
    char name[20];
    float height;  // height in metres
    float weight;  // weight in Kg
};

int main()
{
    person p1 = {"Tony Hawken", 1.75, 74.0};

    // Display contents of p1
    cout << "Name" << "\t\t" << "height (m)" << "\t"
        << "weight (Kg)\n";
    cout << p1.name << "\t" << p1.height << "\t\t"
        << p1.weight << endl;

    // Calculate and display weight to height ratio
    float ratio = p1.weight / p1.height;
    cout << fixed << setprecision(2) << "Ratio = "
        << ratio << endl;

    return 0;
}
```

Notes:

1. Structures can be initialised in the same way as arrays.

2. The statement `person p1 = {"Tony Hawken", 1.75, 74.0};` creates an object called p1 of type person. It then assigns `"Tony hawken"` to `p1.name`, 1.75 to `person.height` and 74.0 to `person.weight`.

There follows another example program, this time parameters are passed using reference variables.

Example 74

```cpp
#include <iostream>
#include <iomanip>
using namespace std;

struct person
{
     char name[20];
     float height;  // height in metres
     float weight;  // weight in Kg
};

void enterdetails(person &);
void displaydetails(person &);

int main()
{
     person p1;

     enterdetails(p1);
     displaydetails(p1);

     // Calculate and display weight to height ratio
     float ratio = p1.weight / p1.height;
     cout << fixed << setprecision(2) << "Ratio = "
          << ratio << endl;

     return 0;
}

void enterdetails(person & p)
{
```

```cpp
        cout << "Enter name : ";
        cin.getline(p.name, 20);
        cout << "Enter height (m) : ";
        cin >> p.height;
        cout << "Enter weight (Kg) : ";
        cin >> p.weight;
}

void displaydetails(person & p)
{
        cout << "Name" << "\t\t" << "height (m)" << "\t"
            << "weight (Kg)\n";
        cout << p.name << "\t" << p.height << "\t\t"
            << p.weight << endl;
}
```

Notes:

1. Two functions are used to process the data in the structure p1.

2. Each of these functions has a **parameter** which is a **reference** to the particular structure.

3. In the case of the `enterdetails()` function, when you update the reference variable, you are really updating the structure that is referenced.

The following version demonstrates that structs can have member functions as well as member data.

Example 75

```cpp
#include <iostream>
#include <iomanip>
using namespace std;

struct person
{
        char name[20];
        float height;   // height in metres
        float weight;   // weight in Kg

        void enterdetails()
        {
```

```
            cout << "Enter name : ";
            cin.getline(name, 20);
            cout << "Enter height (m) : ";
            cin >> height;
            cout << "Enter weight (Kg) : ";
            cin >> weight;
      }

      void displaydetails()
      {
            cout << "Name" << "\t\t" << "height (m)";
            cout << "\t" << "weight (Kg)\n";
            cout << name << "\t" << height;
            cout << "\t\t" << weight << endl;
      }
};

void enterdetails(person &);
void displaydetails(person &);

int main()
{
      person p1;
      p1.enterdetails();
      p1.displaydetails();

      // Calculate and display weight to height ratio
      float ratio = p1.weight / p1.height;
      cout << fixed << setprecision(2) << "Ratio = "
            << ratio << endl;

      return 0;
}
```

Notes:

1. Structure definitions are able to contain functions as well. These are called **member functions** or **methods**.

2. An object of a given data type can use the **member functions** to process the data within a particular object of the given type.

3. The member functions in this program are called by the data object p1. This style of programming is like object-oriented programming. Because the data object calls the function, there is no need to pass any parameters, as the function expects that the data to process, is the data stored within the calling object.

The following program uses a class instead of a structure. The only immediate difference is the presence of the data access control keywords **private:** and **public:** that can be used to determine access.

Example 76

```cpp
#include <iostream>
#include <iomanip>
using namespace std;

class person
{
    private:

    char name[20];
    float height;  // height in metres
    float weight;  // weight in Kg

    public:

    void enterdetails()
    {
        cout << "Enter name : ";
        cin.getline(name, 20);
        cout << "Enter height (m) : ";
        cin >> height;
        cout << "Enter weight (Kg) : ";
        cin >> weight;
    }

    void displaydetails()
    {
        cout << "Name" << "\t\t" << "height (m)";
        cout << "\t" << "weight (Kg)\n";
        cout << name << "\t" << height;
        cout << "\t\t" << weight << endl;
    }

    float ratio()
    {
        return weight / height;
    }

};

int main()
{
    person p1;

    p1.enterdetails();
    p1.displaydetails();
```

```
    // Calculate and display weight to height ratio
    cout << fixed << setprecision(2);
    cout << "Ratio = " << p1.ratio() << endl;

    return 0;
}
```

```
Quincy 2005                                                    _ □ ✕
Enter name : Tony Hawken
Enter height (m) : 1.75
Enter weight (Kg) : 76
Name            height (m)        weight (Kg)
Tony Hawken     1.75              76
Ratio = 43

Press Enter to return to Quincy..._
```

Notes:

1. A **class** is a generalization of a **struct**. Both **class** and **struct**, allow **member data** and **member functions (methods)**

2. A **class**, in addition includes **member-access control**. That is, you can specify whether or not data can be accessed outside the class.

3. The keyword **public** states that an item can be accessed.

4. The keyword **private** states that the item is hidden and cannot be accessed unless an **object** of this type uses a **member function** from this **class**.

5. In this example the **member functions** are **public**. That is they can be accessed from within main().

6. In this example the **member data** is declared to be **private**. They can only be accessed by **member functions** declared in the same class.

7. The statement p1.enterdetails(); is a **function call** that is initiated by the object p1. The function enterdetails() will act on the **member data** within the object p1.

8. A new **member function** ratio() has been written to compute the weight-height ratio. We could not do it the same as for the program in *example 75* as the **member data** is declared to be **private**.

9. This style of programming - that uses both **classes** and **objects** is referred to as **object-oriented** programming. Up until now we have had very little to do with this.

146

Exercise 12-1

1. (a) Write a program that includes the following declaration:

```
struct frac
{
    int n; // numerator
    int d; // denominator
};
```

(b) Include a function to enter data into objects of type frac, and another function to display the current value of a particular fraction object.

(c) Write other functions to add, subtract, multiply and divide two fractions together. Each of these functions should return a value of type frac.

2. (a) Implement a program that has a date structure (dd: mm: yr)

(b) Write functions to both enter member data, and display the values for a given date object

(c) Create two variables of this type – dob (date of birth) and current date.

(d) Write a function to find the persons current age in years and months.

3. (a) Represent a point so that it can be represented as using two numbers of form (x, y) e.g. (3.6, 4.5).

(b) Test this structure by writing a test program that will create two points. This test program will have a function called enterpoint(), that will allow a user to enter the x and y co-ordinates of a point and another function called displaypoint(), that will display the point in the form (4.5, 6.8).

(c) Add a function called distance() that will return the distance between two points.

(d) Add another function called midpoint(), that can return the midpoint of a line specified by two given points.

12.3   Arrays of structures

The following program shows how an array can be used to store a structure.

Example 77

```cpp
#include <iostream>
#include <iomanip>
#include <string>
using namespace std;

struct person
{
    string name;
    float height;  // height in metres
    float weight;  // weight in Kg
};

int main()
{
    person p1[5];  // Create an array of objects of type person

    // Enter details into array
    for(int c = 0; c < 5; c++)
    {
        cout << "Enter name : ";
        getline(cin, p1[c].name);
        cout << "Enter height in metres : ";
        cin >> p1[c].height;
        cout << "Enter weight in Kg : ";
        cin >> p1[c].weight;
        cin.ignore(1000, '\n');
    }

    // Display contents of p1
    cout << "Name" << "\t\t" << "height (m)" << "\t"
        << "weight (Kg)\n";
    for(int c = 0; c < 5; c++)
    {
        cout << p1[c].name << "\t" << p1[c].height << "\t\t";
        cout << p1[c].weight << endl;
    }

    return 0;
}
```

Notes :

1. The statement   person p1[5];   declares an array of 5 objects of type
   person

2. `getline()` is used to read a string that may include whitespace. Note it is a different format of `getline()` as a string object is being read.

3. The expression `p1[4].name` refers to the name field in the 5th object in the array called p1.

4. The statement `cin.ignore(1000, '\n');` is required to skip past all the characters until a **newline** character is detected. The reason for having to use this is that we are reading both strings and numbers from the file. So, there is a need to start at the beginning of a new line ready to read the next string.

```
Quincy 2005

Enter name : Tony Hawken
Enter height in metres : 1.75
Enter weight in Kg : 76
Enter name : Fred Bloggs
Enter height in metres : 1.69
Enter weight in Kg : 78
Enter name : Tom Smith
Enter height in metres : 1.81
Enter weight in Kg : 84
Enter name : Tom James
Enter height in metres : 1.70
Enter weight in Kg : 64
Enter name : Dave Swan
Enter height in metres : 1.78
Enter weight in Kg : 77
Name            height (m)       weight (Kg)
Tony Hawken     1.75             76
Fred Bloggs     1.69             78
Tom Smith       1.81             84
Tom James       1.7              64
Dave Swan       1.78             77

Press Enter to return to Quincy..._
```

Note:

The above output can be produced by both example 72 and example 73.

The following program uses functions to process an array of structures.

Example 78

```cpp
#include <iostream>
#include <iomanip>
#include <string>

struct person
{
    char name[20];
    float height;  // height in metres
    float weight;  // weight in Kg
};

void enterdetails(person &);
void displaydetails(person []);
```

149

```
int main()
{
    person p1[5];  // Create an array of objects of type person

    // Enter details into array
    for(int c = 0; c < 5; c++)
        enterdetails(p1[c]);

    // Display contents of p1
    displaydetails(p1);

    return 0;
}

void enterdetails(person & p)
{
    cout << "Enter name : ";
    gets(p.name);
    cout << "Enter height in metres : ";
    cin >> p.height;
    cout << "Enter weight in Kg : ";
    cin >> p.weight;
}

void displaydetails(person p [])
{
    cout << "Name" << "\t\t" << "height (m)"
        << "\t" << "weight (Kg)\n";
    for(int c = 0; c < 5; c++)
    {
        cout << p[c].name << "\t" << p[c].height << "\t\t";
        cout << p[c].weight << endl;
    }
}
```

Notes:

1. The function `enterdetails()` has one parameter - a reference to an object of type person.

2. The function `displaydetails()` has one parameter - a variable of type array of person. When passing the name of an **array**, you don't need to pass a **reference** because the name of an array is in fact a **reference**.

12.4   Implement fractions using structures

This section implements question 1 from exercise 12-1

To understand this problem, it is necessary to revise some basic mathematics – particularly fractions.

A fraction or rational number is any number that can be represented as one integer divided by another. So $\frac{3}{5}$ is a fraction. Here the 3 is referred to as the numerator, and 5 is the denominator.

Rules of fractions

Addition $\qquad \frac{a}{b} + \frac{c}{d} = \frac{a \times d}{b \times d} + \frac{b \times c}{b \times d} = \frac{a \times d + b \times c}{b \times d}$

Subtraction $\qquad \frac{a}{b} - \frac{c}{d} = \frac{a \times d}{b \times d} - \frac{b \times c}{b \times d} = \frac{a \times d - b \times c}{b \times d}$

Multiplication $\qquad \frac{a}{b} \times \frac{c}{d} = \frac{a \times c}{b \times d}$

Division $\qquad \frac{a}{b} \div \frac{c}{d} = \frac{a}{b} \times \frac{d}{c} = \frac{a \times d}{b \times c}$

We also need to be able to simplify our answers. This is often referred to as cancellation. It involves finding the largest number that divides into the numerator and denominator.

In the program that follows there are two functions for this purpose. The number that divides both the numerator and denominator is called the highest common factor (HCF) or greatest common divisor (gcd) depending on which book you read. You can cancel a fraction by dividing both the numerator and denominator by the gcd.

Example 79

```cpp
#include <iostream>
using namespace std;

struct frac
{
    int n;      // numerator
    int d;      // denominator
};

void enterdata(frac &);
void displaydata(frac &);
int gcd(int, int);
void reduce(frac &);
frac add(frac &, frac &);
frac sub(frac &, frac &);
frac mul(frac &, frac &);
frac div(frac &, frac &);
```

151

```cpp
int main()
{
    frac a, b, c;   // allocate storage for two fractions
    enterdata(a);
    enterdata(b);
    // demonstrate add
    c = add(a, b);
    displaydata(a); cout << " + "; displaydata(b);
    cout << " = "; displaydata(c); cout << endl;
    // demonstrate subtract
    c = sub(a, b);
    displaydata(a); cout << " - "; displaydata(b);
    cout << " = "; displaydata(c); cout << endl;
    // demonstrate multiply
    c = mul(a, b);
    displaydata(a); cout << " * "; displaydata(b);
    cout << " = "; displaydata(c); cout << endl;
    // demonstrate divide
    c = div(a, b);
    displaydata(a); cout << " / "; displaydata(b);
    cout << " = "; displaydata(c); cout << endl;

    return 0;
}

void enterdata(frac & a)
{
    cout << "Enter numerator : ";
    cin >> a.n;
    cout << "Enter denominator : ";
    cin >> a.d;
}

void displaydata(frac & a)
{
    cout << a.n << "/" << a.d;
}

int gcd(int j, int k)
{
    if (k == 0)
        return j;
    else
        return gcd(k, j % k);
}

void reduce(frac & a)
{
    int fac = gcd(a.n, a.d);
    a.n /= fac;
    a.d /= fac;
}
```

```
frac add(frac & a, frac & b)
{
     frac c;
     c.n = a.n * b.d + a.d * b.n;
     c.d = a.d * b.d;
     reduce(c);
     return c;
}

frac sub(frac & a, frac & b)
{
     frac c;
     c.n = a.n * b.d - a.d * b.n;
     c.d = a.d * b.d;
     reduce(c);
     return c;
}

frac mul(frac & a, frac & b)
{
     frac c;
     c.n = a.n * b.n;
     c.d = a.d * b.d;
     reduce(c);
     return c;
}

frac div(frac & a, frac & b)
{
     frac c;
     c.n = a.n * b.d;
     c.d = a.d * b.n;
     reduce(c);
     return c;
}
```

```
Quincy 2005                                              _ □ ×
Enter numerator : 1
Enter denominator : 2
Enter numerator : 3
Enter denominator : 4
1/2 + 3/4 = 5/4
1/2 - 3/4 = 1/-4
1/2 * 3/4 = 3/8
1/2 / 3/4 = 2/3

Press Enter to return to Quincy..._
```

Notes:

1. The function `gcd()` is an example of a recursive function. It uses Euclid's algorithm.

153

2. The function `reduce()` is used to cancel fractions. It finds the HCF (gcd) of the numerator and denominator. It then divides the numerator and denominator by this number.

Exercise 12-2

1.
   (a) Write a program that contains a structure that contains a persons name, and two numbers representing a start time and finish time for a particular days work.

   (b) Create an array that can store at least 10 records with the structure described above.

   (c) Write a function that will allow you to enter the data for each record.

   (d) Write another function that will enable you to display the entire contents of the array.

   (e) Write another function that will work out the average number of hours worked for all of the individuals stored in the array.

2. Referring back to exercise 13.1, it was mentioned that for real roots of a quadratic equation $b^2 = 4ac$. If for any reason $b^2 < 4ac$ then $b^2 - 4ac$ is negative, and if you try and calculate the square root of this you get an error. To get round this problem, mathematicians call this an imaginary number. So if $b^2 - 4ac = -17$, the square root of this is written as 17i. Here i = $\sqrt{(-1)}$. When you combine imaginary numbers with real numbers you end up with complex numbers. A complex number is of the form a + ib. These complex numbers can be combined in similar ways to real numbers.

   Addition $\qquad$ (a + ib) + (c + id) = (a + c) + (b + d)i

   Multiplication $\qquad$ (a + ib)(c + id) = ac + adi + bci + bdi^2

   $\qquad\qquad\qquad\qquad$ = (ac - bd) + (ad + bc)i $\quad$ as i^2 = -1

   Write a program that includes a structure called complex, that has two data items to represent the real and imaginary parts of a complex number. Write functions called `add()` and `mul()` which can be used to add and multiply two complex numbers using the rules above. Test these functions by adding and multiplying complex numbers.

Chapter 13 (Week 13)

13.1 Using Files

For large amounts of data it is not practical to store the data in memory. The data has to be stored on disk, and the container that holds this data is called a file.

The simplest type of file organisation is a text file. A text file is merely a large sequence of characters. It is not unlike text typed in from the keyboard. The main difference is that it can be very much larger. Text files only store text. How this text is interpreted, is determined by the program that reads it.

Certain sequences of characters can be interpreted to be numbers (int, float or double). All numbers need to be separated by one or more spaces – exactly the same as if you enter 3 numbers from the keyboard.

We have already studied stream i/o. So we are already familiar with the stream objects **cout** and **cin** used for output and input respectively. Both of these streams are defined automatically and can be used when you include the header file **<iostream>**

A stream is merely a type of channel connecting variables in memory to a file. Here the word file is being used very loosely, as a file can also refer to an input device such as a keyboard or an output device such as a screen.

To use disk files you need to create additional streams:

1. Input file streams need to be of type **ifstream**

2. Output file streams need to be of type **ofstream**

The classes **ifstream** and **ofstream** are both declared in the header file **<fstream>**.

Once **stream objects** have been created, the object itself can be used to open a given file – either for input or output.

You will also notice that these streams use the same operators as **cin** and **cout** respectively. So learning how to process files is not much more difficult than using the keyboard and screen.

13.2   A simple program to read data from a file

A simple text file can be created using an editor such as notepad. Simply type in the data as you would any text file. Remember to include spaces between each data item.

Creating a data file using a text editor

The following program can be used to read such a text file.

Example 80

```cpp
#include <iostream>
#include <fstream>
using namespace std;

int main()
{    char name[10];
     char a;
     int b;
     float c;
     double d;

     ifstream infile;     // Create an input file-stream object
     infile.open("mydata.txt");     // Open mydata for reading

     // Read the data from file into named variables
     infile >> name;
     infile >> a;
     infile >> b;
     infile >> c;
     infile >> d;

     // Display values input
     cout << "Name = " << name << endl;
     cout << "a = " << a << endl;
     cout << "b = " << b << endl;
     cout << "c = " << c << endl;
     cout << "d = " << d << endl;

     infile.close();     // Close the file mydata

     return 0;
}
```

Output from running program

```
C:\ Quincy 2005                                          _ □ ✕
Name = Tony
a = A
b = 5
c = 12.6
d = 53.9998

Press Enter to return to Quincy...
```

Notes:

1. A data file can be created using any text-editor. In this case notepad was used.

2. The **ifstream** object **infile** is used to open the text file for reading.

3. Once the file is open, you can use the say operators for **infile** as you would **cin**.

4. It is normal practice to close the file once all file-processing is finished. This is done using `infile.close()`.

5. You don't need to close the file in this case, because all files are closed once the program has finished.

13.3   Writing to a file

<u>Example 81</u>

```cpp
#include <iostream>
#include <fstreamh>
using namespace std;

int main()
{
    char name[20];
    int number;
    ofstream outfile;
    outfile.open("mydata.txt");
    cout << "Enter your name : ";
    cin.getline(name, 20);
    outfile << "My name is " << name << endl;
    outfile << "My numbers are ";
    for(int c = 0; c < 10; c++)
    {
        cout << "Enter next number : ";
        cin >> number;
        outfile << number << "   ";
    }
    outfile << endl;
```

```
        outfile.close();
        return 0;
}
```

Running the previous program

Contents of the data file mydata.txt

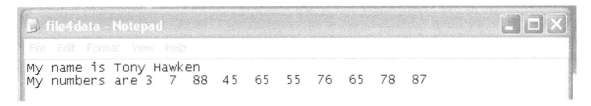

```
file4data - Notepad

File  Edit  Format  View  Help

My name is Tony Hawken
My numbers are 3  7  88  45  65  55  76  65  78  87
```

Notes:

1. An output file-stream is created using the declaration **ofstream outfile;**

2. The string name is written to the file with **outfile << name << endl;**

3. Numbers can be added to the file-stream with **outfile << number;**

4. It is necessary to use spaces to separate the numbers when writing them to a file.

5. If you call the file `myfiledata.txt` instead of `myfiledata`, it will be easier for you to open the file in notepad.

Exercise 13-1

1.

(a) Refer back to section 2.7 and look at example 23. Modify this program so that all input comes from a file. You file should consist of 5 lines created using notepad. On each line there should be 3 numbers, corresponding to the coefficients of a quadratic equation – a, b and c.

(b) Add a test to determine whether a real root is possible for any given set of coefficients. The following information may help.

For a given quadratic equation of form $ax^2 + bx + c = 0$. The coefficients are a, b and c.

The condition for real roots is $b^2 \leq 4ac$

(c) Make sure that the output on the screen is appropriately formatted in the form of a table. The first 3 columns of the table will be the coefficients a, b and c. If the equation has real roots, display the two roots. Otherwise display the message "No real roots".

(d) Modify this version, so that all of these results are output to a file instead. Check the contents of the file to make sure that this has happened.

13.4   Test for success of opening files

<u>Example 82</u>

```cpp
#include <iostream>
#include <fstream>
#include <cstdlib>

using namespace std;

int main(){    string name;           // Name of AS level maths
     int c1, c2, s1;       // Percentage marks for C1, C2 and S1
     char grade;

     //Prepare to read input file
     ifstream fin;
     fin.open("infile.txt");
     if(fin.fail())
     {
          cout << "Could not open file for reading" << endl;
          exit(1);
     }
     else
          cout << "File successfully opened for reading" << endl;

     //Input data from file
     getline(fin, name);
     fin >> c1 >> c2 >> s1;

     //Process data
     float av = (c1 + c2 + s1) / 3.0;
     if(av >= 80)
          grade = 'A';
     else if (av < 80 && av >= 70)
          grade = 'B';
     else if (av < 70 && av >= 60)
          grade = 'C';
     else if (av < 60 && av >= 50)
          grade = 'D';
     else if (av < 50 && av >= 40)
          grade = 'E';
     else if (av < 40)
          grade = 'U';

     //Prepare to write to output file
     ofstream fout;
     fout.open("outfile.txt");
     if (fout.fail())
     {
          cout << "could not open file for writing" << endl;
          exit(1);
     }
     else
```

```
        cout << "File opened for writing" << endl;

    //Output data to file
    fout << name << "C1 = " << c1 << "C2 = " << c2
        << "S1 = " << s1 << endl;
    fout << "Average mark = " << av;
    fout << "grade = " << grade << endl;

    fin.close();
    fout.close();

    return 0;
}
```

The input file – created using notepad

Running the program

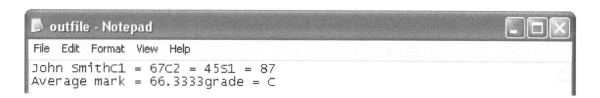

Ouput file created by the program

Notes:

1. The **fstream** member function `fail()` returns true if an error has occurred, false otherwise.

2. The function `fail()` can be used to test both input and output streams.

3. The `exit()` function terminates the program. The parameter 1 is used to denote an error, 0 is usually used for anything else.

4. The **prototype** for `exit()` is found in `<cstdlib>`.

13.5   Appending to the end of a file

The following program uses some of the ios flags. In particular it uses ios::app to open a file in append mode. That way, records can be added to the end of an existing file.

Example 83

```cpp
#include <iostream>
#include <fstream>
using namespace std;


int main()
{
    string name;         //name of person
    int m1, m2, m3;      //marks obtained

    //First file to read from
    ifstream infile1;
    infile1.open("marks1.txt", ios::in);


    //Output file - write records here
    ofstream outfile;
    outfile.open("marks3.txt", ios::out);


    for(int c = 0; c < 3; c++)
    {
        //read a records from first file
        getline(infile1, name);
        infile1 >> m1 >> m2 >> m3;
        infile1.ignore(80, '\n');

        //Output records to another file
        outfile << name << endl;
        outfile << m1 << "\t" << m2 << "\t"<< m3 << endl;
    }

    outfile.close();
    ifstream infile2;
    infile2.open("marks2.txt", ios::in);

    //can now append to end of file
    outfile.open("marks3.txt", ios::app);

    if (outfile)
    {
        cout << "Appending records to end of file" << endl;

        for(int c = 0; c < 2; c++)
```

```
                {
                        //read a records from first file
                        getline(infile2, name);
                        infile2 >> m1 >> m2 >> m3;
                        infile2.ignore(80, '\n');

                        //Output records to another file
                        outfile << name << endl;
                        outfile << m1 << "\t" << m2 << "\t"<< m3 << endl;
                }

        return 0;
}
```

marks1.txt

```
marks2 - Notepad
File  Edit  Format  View  Help
Fiona williams
65   85   91
Owen white
84   35   61
```

marks2.txt

```
marks1 - Notepad
File  Edit  Format  View  Help
Tony Hawken
87   69   92
Fred Smith
45   65   87
Tom Smart
45   34   91
```

marks3.txt

```
marks3 - Notepad
File  Edit  Format  View  Help
Tony Hawken
87          69          92
Fred Smith
45          65          87
Tom Smart
45          34          91
Fiona williams
65          85          91
Owen white
84          35          61
```

163

Notes:

1. When you open a file you can specify an ios flag. This is used to specify the mode of opening a file.

2. The ios flags in and out are redundant in this example, as by default you would expect to get these anyway.

3. The ios flag app is used to append to the end of a file. When you open a file in this mode, all data written to this file will appear after the end of the file.

The technique of appending to the end of a file can be extended to the application of joining two files. In particular we may want to carry out one of the following.

Concatenation is the process of joining two files by appending one file to the end of another file.

Merging is the process of taking two sorted files and interleaving the records according to the sort order of a particular key field. This should result in a sorted file created using the contents of two smaller sorted files. In file maintenance terms merging is a very important feature which we will look at in detail later.

By far the easiest to discuss and implement is concatenation

This involves reading a second file, and appending it contents to the end of the first file. If you want to preserve the contents of the first file, you could start by copying the first file to a third file, and then appending the contents of the second file to the end of the third file. If the latter approach is adopted, you probably won't need to open any files in append mode.

13.5   Process statistical data – file version

The following program is based on example 68, but has been extended read data from a file, and then output the results to a file.

Example 84

```cpp
#include <iostream>
#include <fstream>
#include <iomanip>
#include <cmath>
using namespace std;

struct datarec
{
    char name[20];
    float times[24];
};

void read_rec(ifstream &, datarec &);
void display_rec(datarec &);
void bsort(float [], int);
float mean(datarec &);
float median(datarec &);
float sd(datarec &);
void range(datarec &, float &, float &, float &);

int main()
{
    ifstream infile;
    char filename[10];
    datarec r1; // Only need one record - process
                // a record at a time
    float lq, uq, iqr;  // range variables

    cout << "Enter name of data file : ";
    cin >> filename;
    infile.open(filename);
    int rec_num;    // Number of records in the file
    infile >> rec_num;
    infile.ignore(80,'\n');  // Skip remaining characters on line

    for(int c = 1; c <= rec_num; c++)
    {
        // Process each record
        read_rec(infile, r1);
        bsort(r1.times, 24);      // sort data
        display_rec(r1);          // display record with sorted
                                  // times
        cout << "Mean of this data is " << mean(r1) << endl;
        cout << "Median value of this data is "
             << median(r1) << endl;
```

```cpp
            cout << "Standard deviation = " << sd(r1) << endl;
            range(r1, lq, uq, iqr);
            cout << "Lower quartile = " << lq << endl;
            cout << "Upper quartile = " << uq << endl;
            cout << "Inter-quartile range = " << iqr << endl;
            cout << endl;
        }
        return 0;
}


void read_rec(ifstream & f, datarec & d)
{
        f.getline(d.name, 20);
        f.ignore();    // Skip past end-of-line character
        for(int c = 0; c < 24; c++)
            f >> d.times[c];
        f.ignore();
}

void display_rec(datarec & d)
{
        cout << d.name << endl;
        cout << setw(4) << setprecision(2);
        for(int c = 0; c < 24; c++)
            cout << d.times[c] << "\t";
        cout << endl;
}

void bsort(float a[], int n)
{
        for(int i = 0; i < n; i++)
            for(int j = n-1; j > i; j--)
                if(a[j] < a[j-1])
                {
                    float temp = a[j];
                    a[j] = a[j-1];
                    a[j-1] = temp;
                }
}

float mean(datarec & d)
{
        float sumx = 0.0;
        for(int c = 0; c < 24; c++)
            sumx += d.times[c];
        return (sumx / 24);
}

float median(datarec & d)
{
        float midval = (d.times[11] + d.times[12]) / 2;
        return midval;
```

166

```
}

float sd(datarec & d)
{
    float sumx2 = 0.0;
    for (int c = 0; c < 24; c++)
        sumx2 += d.times[c] * d.times[c];
    float variance = sumx2 / 24 - mean(d) * mean(d);
    return sqrt(variance);
}

void range(datarec & d, float & lq, float & uq, float & iqr)
{
    lq = (d.times[5] + d.times[6]) / 2;
    uq = (d.times[17] + d.times[18]) / 2;
    iqr = uq - lq;
}
```

Data file – can be type in using either notepad or edit (or any other text-editor)

Results file as seen within an editor

```
nazeera - Notepad
File  Edit  Search  Help
4         // Number of records to process
Nazeera
 8.69   12.91   16.81   15.23   14.39   16.49
19.82   20.14   12.26   12.41   13.86   13.22
13.78   12.52   15.29   15.25   12.60   13.24
13.98   13.82   15.95   13.27   13.81   12.67
Jyothi
11.09   11.13   11.95    8.78    7.14    6.79
 7.19    5.77    6.29    5.90    5.63    5.79
 6.29    5.06    6.08    5.04    6.07    5.28
 6.11    6.07    6.05    5.36    7.34    5.03
Johnson
10.42    7.55   10.92    9.52   10.72   10.09
 8.32   10.12   12.72   10.92    9.44   10.52
 6.59   10.57   10.84   12.64   11.00   10.47
 8.90   11.12    9.82   11.23    9.89   10.07
Simon
 8.74   10.50   10.00    7.00   10.30    9.74
 9.86   11.22    9.45   10.78    9.69   10.87
 9.48   10.13   11.35   10.87   11.24   10.90
 9.35   10.10   10.22   10.30   10.76    9.81
```

167

13.6   Read a file using character input

The following program uses character input. The function get(C) will obtain the next character from the file stream. So, a file can be read a character at a time until the end of file marker is detected. In essence the program that follows is merely copying the text from a file to the screen.

Example 85

```cpp
#include <iostream>
#include <fstream>
using namespace std;

int main()
{
    ifstream infile;
    char ch;
    char filename[20];
    cout << "Enter name of file to read : ";
    cin >> filename;
    infile.open(filename);
    while(infile.get(ch))
        cout << ch;
    return 0;
}
```

Output from running above program

Notes:

1. An input file-stream object called infile is created using the statement
   ifstream infile;

2. The **ifstream** class is declared in the header file **fstream.**

3. The class **ifstream** is similar to the class **istream** which is used to declare the **cin** object in **iostream.**

4. A file needs to be opened for input before you can read any data from it. The statement `infile.open(filename);` is used to open a file for reading.

5. The function call `infile.get(ch)` will read the next character from the filestream **infile**. This function call also returns a value that can be used to terminate the while loop. When the end of file character is detected, the loop will terminate.

Exercise 13-2

1.

(a) Write a file application program that uses a struct called film to create a record structure to record information about films in a DVD collection. Each record should include the name, type of film, director and running time in minutes.

(b) There should be functions to add details to a new film object, and to display the contents of such an object.

(c) Extend this program so that the film details corresponding to each film object can be written to a file.

(d) Add functions to write a film object to the end of a file, display the contents of a file, and search for a given record by Director.

(e) Write a function that will produce a menu with 5 options

MENU

1.   Add additional records to a file

2.   Display entire file

3.   Search for a record

4.   Quit Menu

Chapter 14 (Week 14)

In this chapter, I have included a simple assignment. This starts with the specification or assignment brief. There then follows a worked solution that consists mainly of program listings and screen dumps, much in the way that I would expect students to present their work. During this week they are expected to work on their assignment.

14.1   Sample assignment

Assignment for Unit 3

This assignment tests your ability to use Arrays, structs and files

Programming Tasks

Task 1

A level grades are awarded as follows:

Grade A	80-100 %
Grade B	70-79 %
Grade C	60-69%
Grade D	50-59%
Grade E	40-49%
Unclassified	0- 39%

The following test data is to be used for task 1 and task 2.

```
34   47   82   23   76   45   65    9   56   37
73   67   54   49   55   44   42   75   36   53
```

(a) Write a program that allows a user to enter the above data using a keyboard and will then store it in an array. Save the program as Task1.

(b) Add some code to the program called Task1 so that the contents of the array are displayed on the screen. Don't forget to save the program.

(c) Extend this program, so that the last part of the program will calculate the frequency of each grade and display the results in the form of a table. Save this program again.

Task 2

(a) Using notepad, type in the above test data and save the file as mydata.txt.

(b) Write a program called Task2 that will read the data stored in mydata.txt, and will then display the contents on the screen.

(c) Extend this program so that the frequency of each grade is calculated and displayed on the screen.

(d) Now modify this program, so that the frequency of each grade is written to a file called freq.txt.

Task 3

(a) Using notepad, type in the following test data, and save the file as marks.txt.

```
Colmerauer, A
92   37   65
Hopper, G
73   56   45
Kemeny, J
78   56   45
Kernighan, D
56   59   83
Ritchie, D
60   78   89
Stroustrup, B
49   64   76
Wirth, N
87   74   82
```

(b) Write a program that can read this file and display the contents on the screen. Save this program as Task3B.

(c) Modify this program so that it includes a record structure that can store a name and 3 integers.

(d) Using this record structure create an array of these records, so that the entire file can be stored in the array.

(e) Modify your last task, so that instead of assuming that there are 7 records in the file, we have to instead test for end-of-file, to determine when to stop reading records into the array of records.

(f) For each of the tasks above save your modified programs.

Task 4

(a) Starting with the program written for Task 3E, save it as Task4A. Now rewrite the program so that there are two functions. You can use cut-and-paste to do some of this.

1. Write a function called `readRecord()`, that will read a single record from the file and store it in the current position in the array. First time round, the index will be 0. Use it to read all the records from the file.

2. Write a function called displayRecord(), that will display a single record from the array of records onto the screen. Use it to display all of the records.

(b) Save your program Task4A as Task4B. Now add3 more functions. Each function should be tested by displaying the contents of the array at each stage, to demonstrate the functions work.

1. Write a function called `changeMarks()`, that will allow you to change all the marks for a given record.

2. Write a function called `addRecord()`, that will allow you to add a new record to the end of the array.

3. Write a function called `writeToFile()`, that will write a record from the array to a named file. Use this function to write the entire contents of the array to a given file.

Documentation required

1. A program listing for each task completed.

2. At least one screen dump for each task completed.

3. A screen dump of each data file.

4. Include adequate comments in the programs to document them. For task 4, it is expected that each function will have at least one comment. Also, there should be a comment for each part of the program that needs explaining.

14.2   Task1

Program listing Task 1

<u>Example 86</u>

```cpp
#include <iostream>
using namespace std;

int main()
{
    int marks[20];

    // Store 20 numbers in array
    cout << "Entering numbers from keyboard" << endl;
    for(int i = 0; i < 20; i++)
    {
        cout << "Enter next number : ";
        cin >> marks[i];
    }

    //  Display contents of array
    cout << endl << "The numbers stored are" << endl;
    for(int i = 0; i < 20; i++)
        cout << marks[i] << "\t";
    cout << endl;

    // Determine frequency for each grade
    int a = 0, b = 0, c = 0, d = 0, e = 0, u = 0;
    for(int i = 0; i < 20; i++)
        if (marks[i] >= 80)
            a++;
        else if (marks[i] >= 70 && marks[i] < 80)
            b++;
        else if (marks[i] >= 60 && marks[i] < 70)
            c++;
        else if (marks[i] >= 50 && marks[i] < 60)
            d++;
        else if (marks[i] >= 40 && marks[i] < 50)
            e++;
        else
            u++;

    // display frequency of grades
    cout << "grade" << "\t" << "frequency" << endl;
    cout << "A" << "\t" << a << endl;
    cout << "B" << "\t" << b << endl;
    cout << "C" << "\t" << c << endl;
    cout << "D" << "\t" << d << endl;
    cout << "E" << "\t" << e << endl;
    cout << "U" << "\t" << u << endl;
```

```
        return 0;
}
```

screen dump for task1

14.3   Task2

Program listing Task 2

<u>Example 87</u>

```cpp
#include <iostream>
#include <fstream>
using namespace std;

int main()
{
    int marks[20];

    ifstream infile;
    infile.open("mydata.txt");

    //input data into array
    for(int i = 0; i < 20; i++)
    infile >> marks[i];

    // Display data
    cout << "Data input from file" << endl;
    for(int i = 0; i < 20; i++)
        cout << marks[i] << "\t";
    cout << endl;

    // Calculate frequencies
    int a = 0, b = 0, c = 0, d = 0, e = 0, u = 0;
    for(int i = 0; i < 20; i++)
        if (marks[i] >= 80) a++;
        else if(marks[i] >= 70 && marks[i] <= 79) b++;
        else if(marks[i] >= 60 && marks[i] <= 69) c++;
        else if(marks[i] >= 50 && marks[i] <= 59) d++;
        else if(marks[i] >= 40 && marks[i] <= 49) e++;
        else u++;

    // write frequencies to file freq.dat
    ofstream outfile;
    outfile.open("freq.txt");
    outfile << "grade" << "\t" << "freq" << endl;
    outfile << "A" << "\t" << a << endl;
    outfile << "B" << "\t" << b << endl;
    outfile << "C" << "\t" << c << endl;
    outfile << "D" << "\t" << d << endl;
    outfile << "E" << "\t" << e << endl;
    outfile << "U" << "\t" << u << endl;

    infile.close();
    outfile.close();
```

```
        return 0;
}
```

```
C:\Program Files\quincy\bin\quincy.exe                        _ □ ×
Data input from file
34      47      82      23      76      45      65      9       56      37
73      67      54      49      55      44      42      75      36      53

Press Enter to return to Quincy...
```

screen dump for task2

```
freq - Notepad
File  Edit  Format  View  Help
grade   freq
A       1
B       3
C       2
D       4
E       5
U       5
```

screen dump of freq.txt

14.4   Task 3

Screen dump Task 3A

```
marks - Notepad
File  Edit  Format  View  Help
Colmerauer, A
92   37   65
Hopper, G
73   56   45
Kemeny, J
78   56   45
Kernighan, D
56   59   83
Ritchie, D
60   78   89
Stroustrup, B
49   64   76
Wirth, N
87   74   82
```

Listing Task 3B

Example 88

```cpp
#include <iostream>
#include <fstream>

using namespace std;

int main()
{
    string name;
    int m1, m2, m3;
    ifstream infile;
    infile.open("marks.txt");
    for(int c = 1; c <= 7; c++)
    {
        // Input a record
        getline(infile, name);
        infile >>  m1 >> m2 >> m3;
        infile.ignore(80, '\n');
        // Output a record
        cout << name << "\t" << m1 << "\t" << m2 << "\t"
            << m3 << endl;
    }
    return 0;
}
```

Screen dump (same output for Tasks 3B-3D)

```
Quincy 2005
Colmerauer, A    92       37       65
Hopper, G        73       56       45
Kemeny, J        78       56       45
Kernighan, D     56       59       83
Ritchie, D       60       78       89
Stroustrup, B    49       64       76
Wirth, N         87       74       82

Press Enter to return to Quincy...
```

Notes:

1. Ideally there should have been a test to see whether the file had successfully opened.

2. The `getline()` function is used to read a string into name. It is required because there is a space in the name.

3. The `ignore()` function is used after each record has been read, so that spaces can be skipped, ready to read the next name.

Listing Task 3C

<u>Example 89</u>

```cpp
#include <iostream>
#include <fstream>
using namespace std;

struct marks_rec
{
    string name;
    int m1, m2, m3;
};

int main()
{
    marks_rec records[10];

    ifstream infile;
    infile.open("marks.txt");

    //Read file into array of records
    for(int c = 0; c < 7; c++)
    {
        // Input a record
        getline(infile, records[c].name);
        infile >> records[c].m1 >> records[c].m2
                >> records[c].m3;
```

178

```
        infile.ignore(80, '\n');
    }

    for(int c = 0; c < 7; c++)
    {
        // Output a record
        cout << records[c].name << "\t";
        cout << records[c].m1 << "\t" << records[c].m2;
        cout << "\t" << records[c].m3 << endl;
    }

    return 0;
}
```

Notes:

1. In this version data from the file is read into an array of records. The structure of each record is determined by the struct marks_rec.

Listing Task 3D

Example 90

```
#include <iostream>
#include <fstream>
using namespace std;

struct marks_rec
{
    string name;
    int m1, m2, m3;
};

int main()
{
    marks_rec records[10];

    ifstream infile;
    infile.open("marks.txt");

    //Read file into array of records
    int rec_count = 0;
    while(! infile.eof())
    {
        // Input a record
        getline(infile, records[rec_count].name);
        infile >>  records[rec_count].m1
                >> records[rec_count].m2
                 >> records[rec_count].m3;
        infile.ignore(80, '\n');
        rec_count++;    //Last value contains end-of-file
```

```
        }
        rec_count--; //Set count back to last record

        //Display records
        for(int n = 0; n < rec_count; n++)
        {    // Output a record
             cout << records[n].name << "\t";
             cout << records[n].m1 << "\t" << records[n].m2;
             cout << "\t" << records[n].m3 << endl;
        }

        return 0;
}
```

Notes:

1. The main change in this version of the program, is that the function `eof()` is used to detect the end-of-file. This test is at the head of a while loop.

2. Every time a record is read, it is necessary to increment the number of records read. In this case rec_count.

14.5 Task4

Program listing task 4A

Example 91

```cpp
#include <iostream>
#include <fstream>
using namespace std;

struct marks_rec
{
    string name;
    int m1, m2, m3;
};

void readRecord(ifstream &, marks_rec &);
void DisplayRecord(marks_rec &);

int main()
{
    marks_rec records[10];

    ifstream infile;
    infile.open("marks.txt");

    //Read file into array of records
    int rec_count = 0;
    while(! infile.eof())
    {
        readRecord(infile, records[rec_count]);
        rec_count++;
    }

    rec_count--;    //Last record contained end-of-file

    //Display records in array
    for(int n = 0; n < rec_count; n++)
        DisplayRecord(records[n]);

    return 0;
}

void readRecord(ifstream & infile, marks_rec & record)
{
    // Input a record
    getline(infile, record.name);
    infile >> record.m1
           >> record.m2
           >> record.m3;
    infile.ignore(80, '\n');
}
```

```cpp
void DisplayRecord(marks_rec & record)
{
        // Output a record
        cout << record.name << "\t";
        cout << record.m1 << "\t" << record.m2;
        cout << "\t" << record.m3 << endl;
}
```

Program listing Task 4B

<u>Example 92</u>

```cpp
#include <iostream>
#include <fstream>
using namespace std;

struct marks_rec
{
    string name;
    int m1, m2, m3;
};

void readRecord(ifstream &, marks_rec &);
void DisplayRecord(marks_rec &);
void changeMarks(marks_rec &);
void addRecord(marks_rec &);
void writeRecord(ofstream &, marks_rec);

int main()
{
    marks_rec records[10];

    ifstream infile;
    infile.open("marks.txt");

    //Read file into array of records
    int rec_count = 0;
    while(! infile.eof())
    {
        readRecord(infile, records[rec_count]);
        rec_count++;
    }

    rec_count--;    //Last record contained end-of-file

    //Display records in array
    for(int n = 0; n < rec_count; n++)
        DisplayRecord(records[n]);

    //Change a record
    int rec_num;
```

182

```cpp
        cout << "Enter number of record to change ";
        cin >> rec_num;
        changeMarks(records[rec_num]);

        //Add a new record
        addRecord(records[rec_count++]);

        //Display records in array
        for(int n = 0; n < rec_count; n++)
            DisplayRecord(records[n]);


        ofstream outfile;
        outfile.open("task4.txt");

        //Write contents of array to a new file
        for(int n = 0; n < rec_count; n++)
            writeRecord(outfile, records[n]);

        return 0;
}

void readRecord(ifstream & infile, marks_rec & record)
{
    // Input a record
    getline(infile, record.name);
    infile >> record.m1
            >> record.m2
             >> record.m3;
    infile.ignore(80, '\n');
}

void DisplayRecord(marks_rec & record)
{
        // Output a record
        cout << record.name << "\t";
        cout << record.m1 << "\t" << record.m2;
        cout << "\t" << record.m3 << endl;

}

void changeMarks(marks_rec & record)
{
    //Display current record
    cout << endl << "*********Changing marks**********" << endl;
    DisplayRecord(record);
    char ans;
    cout << "Is this the correct record to modify? [y/n] ";
    cin >> ans;
    if (ans == 'y')
    {
        cout << "Enter new first mark : ";
        cin >> record.m1;
```

```cpp
            cout << "Enter new second mark : ";
            cin >> record.m2;
            cout << "Enter new third mark : ";
            cin >> record.m3;
            cout << endl;
        }

}

void addRecord(marks_rec & record)
{
    cout << endl << "Adding a new record" << endl;
    cout << "Enter full name, surname first : ";
    cin.ignore();
    getline(cin, record.name);
    cout << "Enter first mark : ";
    cin >> record.m1;
    cout << "Enter second mark : ";
    cin >> record.m2;
    cout << "Enter third mark : ";
    cin >> record.m3;
    cout << endl;
}

void writeRecord(ofstream & outfile, marks_rec record)
{
    //Write a record
    outfile << record.name << "\t"
            << record.m1 << "\t"
            << record.m2 << "\t"
            << record.m3 << "\t"
            << endl;
}
```

Screen dump for Task 4B

```
C:\Program Files\quincy\bin\quincy.exe

Colmerauer, A      92        37        65
Hopper, G          73        56        45
Kemeny, J          78        56        45
Kernighan, D       56        59        83
Ritchie, D         60        78        89
Stroustrup, B      49        64        76
Wirth, N           87        74        82
Enter number of record to change 2

*********Changing marks**********
Kemeny, J          78        56        45
Is this the correct record to modify? [y/n] y
Enter new first mark : 75
Enter new second mark : 85
Enter new third mark : 95


Adding a new record
Enter full name, surname first : Hawken, Tony
Enter first mark : 87
Enter second mark : 84
Enter third mark : 92

Colmerauer, A      92        37        65
Hopper, G          73        56        45
Kemeny, J          75        85        95
Kernighan, D       56        59        83
Ritchie, D         60        78        89
Stroustrup, B      49        64        76
Wirth, N           87        74        82
Hawken, Tony       87        84        92

Press Enter to return to Quincy..._
```

Screen dump for outfile

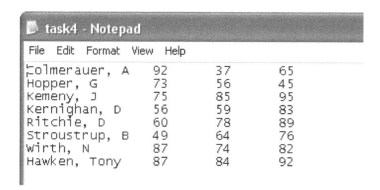

```
task4 - Notepad

File   Edit   Format   View   Help

Colmerauer, A      92        37        65
Hopper, G          73        56        45
Kemeny, J          75        85        95
Kernighan, D       56        59        83
Ritchie, D         60        78        89
Stroustrup, B      49        64        76
Wirth, N           87        74        82
Hawken, Tony       87        84        92
```

Chapter 15 (Week 15)

15.1   Tasks to do

This week is reserved for finishing off your assignment

15.2   End of unit summary

1. An array is a list of consecutive memory locations used to store data of the same type.

2. The declaration **int x[10];** will allocate storage big enough for 10 integers, and the name x will point to the start of this storage.

3. Elements of an array can be accessed by means of a subscript or index. For example **cout << numbers[4] << endl;** will display the 5th element of an array called numbers.

4. Arrays are commonly processed using for loops. This is the case, because it is easy to work out in advance how many items there are in an array. Also, there are many situations where you want to do the same thing to each element.

5. C++ does not prevent you trying to access pass the end of array. That is, there is no array bound checking – it is up to the programmer to make sure that this does not happen. This can be extremely as you could write data in some other memory location, that is occupied by another variable or array.

6. An array of type char can be used to represent a character string. These are referred to as c-strings.

7. An array can be passed to a function by passing the name of the array. There is no need to use a reference because the name of an array is a reference to a memory location where the start of the array is stored.

8. Arrays can be searched. Linear search is the easiest algorithm to implement – here each element of the array is compared in order until a match is found.

9. Arrays can also be sorted. The simplest sorting algorithm is the bubble sort. It is also the slowest.

10.   The keyword struct is used to create a new data type that corresponds to a record structure. It is used to group together a number of data items that are possibly of a different data type.

11. A struct declaration creates a new data type. It can be used to create storage in the same way that you create variables using the primitive data types.

12. Member data items are accessed using the list operator (.). For example **a.name** refers to the data item called name within the object called a.

13. Like a class, a struct can also include member functions (methods) that are used to operate on the member data.

14. In addition, classes also use the keywords **public:** and **private:**. These are used to specify the type of access permitted for elements of the structure.

15. C++ treats all files as a sequential stream of bytes. It should be noted that the keyboard and screen of a computer are treated in the same way, as they too are considered to be files.

16. The header file <fstream> is required if you want to read from a file or write to a file.

17. To access a file, you first have to create a file stream object to open the file.

18. Files are opened for reading using an ifstream object, and are opened for writing using an ofstream object.

19. An **ifstream** object called infile, can be used in the same way as stream object **cin** is used to input data from the keyboard. For example, if x and y are of type int, the statement **infile >> x >> y;** will read the first two integers from the file and store them in x and y respectively.

20. An ofstream object called outfile, can be used in the same way as cout is used to write to the screen.

21. Output files can be opened in append mode, by using the ios flag app. This will allow to write at the end of a file rather than the beginning.

Bibliography

The following bibliography is indicative of the types of books you should be having a look at for further reading. In many cases, the books that follow have been used by the author.

C++ books

Ammeraal, Leen. C++ for programmers 3/e. Wiley 2000

Deitel, H. M & Deitel, P.J. C++: How to program 4/e. Prentice-Hall 2003

Glassborow, Francis. You can program in C++: A programmer's introduction. Wiley 2006

Horton, Ivor. Ivor Horton's Beginning ANSI C++: The complete language 3/e. Apress 2004

Hubbard, John R. Programming with C++ 2/e. (Schaum's outline). McGraw-Hill 2000

Hubbard, John R. Fundamentals of computing with C++ 1/e. (Schaum's outline) McGraw-Hill 1998

Malik, D.S. C++ Programming: From Problem Analysis to Program Design 3/e. Thomson/Course Technology 2007

Stroustrup, Bjarne. Programming: Principles and Practice using C++. Addison Wesley 2009

Other Programming languages

Hawken, Tony. A course in programming with QBASIC. Harbin Engineering University press 1995.

General computing books

French, C. S. Computer Science 5/e. DP publications 1996

Knott, Geoffrey & Waites, Nick. BTEC Nationals in Computing. Brancepeth 2000

Knott, Geoffrey & Waites, Nick. Computing 3/e. Business Education publishers 2000

Index

A

access control 145-146
accessing structure members 139, 141, 187
algorithm 123
AND (&&) 25, 40-41
ANSI standard (C++) 3, 61
append to end of file 162-164
array 105, 109-121
array of structures 148-150
arguments (See parameters)
arithmetic operators 3, 26, 28-29
ASCII code 23, 24, 42
ssignment 11, 24, 27-28
assignment operators 26, 28
assignment statement 11, 24, 28
associativity of operators 29

B

binary 23, 38
binary digit (bit) 23
binary operators 26
binary search 118
binomial theorem 87
bisection search 134
block 4, 13, 61
bool 23, 24, 25
boolalpha 43
boolean expressions 40-43, 44
break statement 49-50, 74, 85, 117, 121
bubble sort 134-136
byte 11, 20, 23, 32

C

C++ 3
call by value 82, 85
call by reference 89-90
calling functions 72, 84-85, 122
case 49-50
casting 66-67
cerr 45-46
char 23, 32, 50

character arrays (c-string) 128
character constant 24
cin 11, 15, 30, 39
class 3
climits 33
close() 156-157
cmath 36, 81-83
comment 8, 10, 31, 37-38, 62
compile program 2, 8
compile time errors 18-19
compiler 2
complex numbers 154
concatenation 15
conditional statements 43-49
const 24
control variable 65, 68
cout 4-5
cstdlib 115
c-string 61, 128

D

data terminator 76, 79
data types 23, 32
debugger 2
debugging 99
dec 39
declaration of functions
declaration of variables 11, 24
decrement operator (--) 28
default (switch statement) 50
do loop 76-78
double 23, 29, 32
dry run 58

E

editor 2
else 43-45
endl 4-5
eof()
equality operator (==) 40-41
errors 1, 8, 18-21
evaluation 59, 141
exit() 116

extraction operator (<<) 4, 10

F

factorial 69, 75, 87, 93-94
`fail()` 140-141
false 23, 40-41
files 136-146
file streams
float 23, 29
for loops 64-68, 70-71
fractions 147, 151-154
fstream 155, 187
      ifstream 155-157, 168-169,
              187
      ofstream 155, 157-158, 187
function 81-95, 122-123
function call 82, 84-85
function definition 84-85, 89, 122
function prototype 82-85
functions that process arrays 113
functions that return void 88

G

Generic programming 3
`getline()` 16-17, 55, 61
global scope 12-13, 62
global variables 12-13, 62, 88-89

H

header files 3
      climits 33
      cmath 36, 78
      cstdlib 115
      fstream 155, 187
      iomanip 37-38
      iostream 3-4, 11
      string 14-16

I

IDE 2, 5
if statement 43-46
if ... else 43-46
ifstream 155-157, 168-169, 187
`ignore()` 148-149, 165
increment operator (++) 28

indentation 5
index (arrays) 125, 135
insertion operator (>>) 11, 15, 17
int 11, 23
integer 23
integer division 27, 30
integer operators 26-27
integer overflow 20
iomanip 37-38
ios 162-164
`ios::app` 162, 164
iostream 3-4, 11

J

JSP 98-99, 107-110, 123

K

Keywords 25

L

left associative 29
`length()` 15, 16, 45
linear search 133-134
link time errors 19
linker (Build) 8
literals 4, 5, 8, 15
local scope 13-14
local variables 13-14
logical expressions 37-38
logic error 21
long 23, 32
long double 23, 32
loop

M

machine code 2, 8
`main()` 4
manipulators 37-39 , 61
mantissa 75
mathematical functions 83
`max()` 86
member data 139, 141, 143, 146,
              187
member function 143-145
method 143-145

U

unsigned 23
using namespace 6

V

variable 11, 32
variable declaration 11, 24
variable assignment 24
verification 46
void 81, 88

W

wchar_t 23
while loop 72-73
white space 17, 30

www.ingramcontent.com/pod-product-compliance
Lightning Source LLC
Chambersburg PA
CBHW081226050326
40689CB00016B/3692